D0666874

George Yates has written a practical, easy to follow guide for those who desire to assist churches to move to the next level through coaching. George has led Coaching seminars for me for years. His simple, easygoing temperament betrays his wealth of experience, wisdom and intellect. In my opinion, his humble and sincere way of coaching churches is exactly what most of our churches need. He has been able to put into words his modest approach so that leaders in any size church can learn and implement these skills into their personal and professional ministry in and through the church. This is a must read for any Pastor, leader or coach who is ready to move their people to the next level. *Sean P. Keith, Sunday School/Discipleship Strategist, Louisiana Baptist Convention*

George Yates is a master at asking questions. Even before Reading, *Coaching: A Way of Leadership a Way of Life,* I have seen first-hand how coaching can radically change the culture within a church, his coaching helped change ours! George masterfully uses the art of asking the right questions, to lead churches and people on a road to self-discovery, helping them identify the God-given purpose for their church. The principles taught in this book, are highly practical and transferable to any setting. They reveal the personal insights of an effective coach with decades of experience. If you have a desire to revolutionize the way you lead in your professional or church life, you need to read this book! *R. Jason Price, Senior Pastor, Cornerstone Baptist Church, Nicholasville, KY.*

George Yates brings fresh insight into coaching conversations through his experiences in business and ministry. This book provides great tools for sharpening your listening skills and a wealth of resource about developing and using questions effectively. George pulls it all together in some practical examples. Coaching: A Way of Leadership, A Way of Life is an excellent resource for anyone looking for practical help in working with people, leaders or leadership teams. *Tom Belew, Consultant, Healthy Church Group, California Southern Baptist Convention*

George Yates' latest book, reminds me of the lyrics of John Fogerty's song "Centerfield" and I must say, "Put me in coach, I'm ready to play today!" I have known George and have read and used everything he has written to improve my performance as a leader. Regardless of your profession, this book will help you to become a better listener, learner and most of all a leader! I encourage you to join George on the path of self-discovery and a better way of life! *Dr. Larry Cheek, Associational Missionary, Stone Mountain Baptist Association of Churches*

Coaching is about relationships so interpersonal skill development is crucial for those who want do it well. This book identifies practical ways to improve listening skills and other vital tools for shaping leaders. As you implement these insights, not only will you learn to coach others, but the book itself will coach you to greater leadership effectiveness. *Jeff Iorg, President, Gateway Seminary*

This book introduces coaching, while simultaneously adding the richness of George's years of experience and expertise as a coach. New and seasoned coaches alike will find this book helpful. George expertly covers the topics of listening and questions throughout this book. Leaders will benefit by learning the importance of listening to the eyes, face, shoulders, arms and hands of others. Add to this, the practical teaching on the formation of powerful questions, which is invaluable. My favorite part is the section on eye movement – horizontal and vertical. This book is ideal for the leader that is looking for a solid biblical approach to coaching. The practical insights contained in these pages will be a significant resource for all of today's leaders. Thank you, George, for this outstanding resource. *J. Val Hastings, Master Certified Coach, Coaching 4 Clergy*

George, Yates has written a very good book on Coaching that deals with the kinds of things every coach will need to apply. Every person interested in coaching others needs to read this book. It is thorough, practical and very applicable to real life coaching. I will use it in my Revitalization strategy. *Larry Wynn, Vice President, Church Revitalization and Evangelism, Georgia Baptist Mission Board*

More resources from George Yates and SonC.A.R.E. Ministries

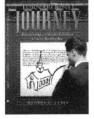

Turnaround Journey: Discovering a Path for Effective leadership Embedded in this story are important principles about actually leading an organization to plan and implement strategic change. Many churches & organizations plan, but there is large difference between planning and strategic planning for implementation and effective results. Learn more at: http://soncare.net/turnaround-journey/

Reaching the Summit: Avoiding and Reversing Decline in the Church – Straight forward, practical, this book is a down to earth analysis of why so many churches are in decline and what to do about it. Methodically works through the five phases of decline the book then turns to the process of identifying the principles and strategies for "Reversing and Avoiding Decline." Learn more at: http://soncare.net/reaching-the-summit/

Teaching That Bears Fruit is teaching that produces true learning – life changing learning. This work looks at the methods

Jesus used to create lasting learning in His listeners. Powerful enough to turn the world upside down. Jesus' teachings are still transforming lives more than 2,000 years later. An indispensable book for anyone who loves to teach the Bible. Learn more at: http://soncare.net/teaching-that-bears-fruit/

SSLES -Sunday School Leader Equipping Series – A CD with a year's worth of equipping sessions for Bible study leaders. 10 complete lessons with Leaders Guide to teach the session, learners handouts, and PowerPoint presentations. Also, additional information to conduct monthly training sessions. Learn more at: http://soncare.net/sunday-school-leader-equipping-sessions/

COACHING

A Way of Leadership

A Way of Life

George L. Yates

Unless otherwise noted all scripture is from the Holman
Christian Standard Bible (HCSB), copyright © 1999, 2000,
2002, 2003, 2009 by Holman Bible Publishers.

Published by Sonlight Publishing
USA

SonC.A.R.E. Ministries
Christ's Awareness Raised Everyday
Web: soncare.net

ISBN: 978-0-9988852-0-9

Printed by: CreateSpace

Table of Contents

Introduction

Why a Coach?

Coaching has become a buzz word the last 10-12 years. But what is a coach and why should people be interested in using a coach? First off, the type of coach we are referring to is a person from the outside; someone who has no bias to your current reality or situation. I had a pastor sitting in a group with 67 of his peers, all came freely to this workshop because their churches were in decline. This pastor, sitting in the middle of the room asked, "Why do I need a coach? Why can't I do that on my own?"

My reply to this pastor and to all 68 men and women in the room was, "How is that working for you so far?" Think about it. This pastor was saying, "We know things are not as healthy as they should be in our church (my wording is probably mild to the actual situation). We know we need to make some changes." What he was asking was, "Why can't I and the leaders of my church who have been leading my church for the past ten years, why can't we do that without a coach?"

There are several reasons why a coach is a benefit. First, a coach is *not* someone who comes in with all the answers. A coach is an experienced listener who uses stories, illustrations, and questions to lead and guide the coachee (individual or team) in determining the proper course of action for moving forward. There are no cookie cutter, pre-packed boxed approaches. The objective of the coach is to elicit strategies and solutions from those being coached.

A coach is someone from the outside. A person who has the coachee's best interest at heart, who wants the coachee (individual or organization) to reach for his/her greatest

1

potential. An outside coach is a person who will walk with the individual, church, or other organization through the coaching and planning process.

Without the assistance of an outside coach an individual or organization will have a tendency to lean on and live in the past, not willing to undertake the sometimes-arduous task of needed change. We all work out of our experience and knowledge base. It is difficult to strive toward something of which we have no knowledge base. To reach for our potential means to be stretched out of our comfort zone.

Without an outside coach an individual or organization will steer away from finding resolution to difficult situations, touchy issues, and traditional trends related to the reality of our current situation. We all view our ministry through our own bias. A coach is someone from the outside who has no bias of our situation and current reality.

Leading to Discovery

A coach is one who leads people to discovery. It is not often that a person will realize his/her potential without the help and encouragement of others. A coach helps individuals and teams to realize their potential and to discover ways of being efficient and effective in reaching that God-given potential. Most often when we think of a coach we think of sports teams. There is at least one similarity between these two types of coaches.

There has never been a sports coach who gave one once of skill to an athlete. A sports coach cannot endow or give an athlete any skill or ability to be a better ball player or athlete. You cannot give skill. What the great sports coaches have learned to do is assist the player in discovering and developing the skill and ability that lies inside the athlete. Thus, challenging the athlete to rise to his/her full potential as a ball player, runner, or swimmer.

Similarly, a personal coach assists the coachee in discovering and developing the life skills and abilities he/she has inside, allowing him/her to rise to his/her full potential in business and in life.

Not only in business and ministry, today people are using coaches for academic purposes, health related issues, family and personal coaching. One of the great attributes of coaching is that the skills and abilities worked on in one area of life tend to transfer over to other areas of life as well bringing balance and satisfaction.

At SonC.A.R.E. Ministries we believe in people, and we want to see everyone reach for his/her potential. As a life coach, our approach is always about the best interest of our client, the coachee. It is our belief that this will assist our clients, be it individuals or teams, in being better, and more well balanced persons in all of life's arenas.

I began coaching years before life coaching was recognized as a form of leadership. About ten years ago, I hired a professional coach to come and spend two days training pastors and church leaders in our region, in the basics of coaching. He arrived in town a day early and we spent several hours together sightseeing. Throughout the day, he would look at me and say, "You already use coaching, don't you?" or some similar statement or question.

I had never really given it much thought, but considering his query and compliments, I realized, I had moved to a coaching style leadership and training model several years prior to our conversation. Since that day, I have turned my focus each year to intentionally becoming a better coach.

For the past five years, I have not only coached individuals, teams, and churches, I have been training others to develop coaching skills in their lives, ministry, and business. I do not consider myself to have arrived at being the best coach available. Nor do I believe I have arrived at my full potential. What I do have to offer is nearly twenty years of experience and thirty-five years of study and learning the techniques and practices of great quality coaching leadership.

There are, what I consider, two major quality characteristics of coaching. Without continually striving to increase your understanding and use of these two characteristics, one will never be a coach of great value. I began to understand the value of these two characteristics as a very young adult. At that time, I had no idea where my journey would lead me. I began studying them simply to better myself as a salesman. Wow! What a journey it has been. To God be the glory.

Two Quality Characteristics of a Worthy Coach

A worthy coach demonstrates exemplary listening skills and has the ability to formulate good, open-ended, thought provoking questions that will assist in moving the coachee forward. For every coach the <u>discipline</u> to carefully listen without interrupting with an answer, advice, or suggestion is a learned skill. When it is time to speak, a worthy coach will be able to formulate a question that will engage the higher level thought processes of the coachee. A proper line of questions will always lead the coachee toward forward progress in his/her life.

Being able to formulate the proper questions for every situation is the first characteristic of a worthy coach. Questions are used every day by each one of us. In much of life we are either asking or answering questions. The shortcoming is that most often the questions being asked are the wrong questions. Therefore, we spend much of our time formulating the wrong answers.

Most of the questions we ask are the wrong questions. As leaders and teachers (we're all leading, teaching someone) we should never ask a question that does not have as its intent to move the individual or organization forward toward his potential.

I have been a student of the question for more than thirty-five years. Chapter four of *Teaching That Bears Fruit*, my first book, is titled "*The Art of The Question*" and I have written several articles and blog posts over the years on formulating and using questions. Yet, I still push myself to learn more, how to be more intentional with questions. How to assist others in reaching their potential using properly formulated questions. My quest is not merely for me to gain knowledge. It is to be better equipped to assist other individuals and organizations.

The chapters dealing with questions in this book will assist you in becoming a more intentional coach; one who truly assists the coachee in discovering and developing a plan of action that belongs to her, not based on your experience. No matter your background, you can learn how to formulate good thought-provoking questions to move the person or organization forward.

In coaching, it is difficult to ask the properly formulated questions without understanding the person or organization sitting in front of you. You must be a good listener. This is the second characteristic of a worthy coach. Listening as a coach requires much more than the basic skills you have ascertained in life. Most of our normal listening is done with our ears and has as its purpose to be able to formulate a response from our own experience and knowledge base.

The words you use make up only seven (7) percent of what you communicate. Therefore, as coaches, we must learn to listen with more than our ears. The chapters in this book dealing with listening will assist you in understanding and practicing listening with all five of your senses.

While coaching consists of more than listening and formulating proper questions, without these as a baseline, you will never achieve a quality level of coaching. Without a quality level of coaching, your coachees will never reach their potential. Coaching leadership has rendered some of the greatest rewards of my life. My prayer is that no man or woman will ever enter the coaching arena without a commitment to continually strive to improve in these two fields.

We will touch other characteristics of coaching as well in the pages of this book. But the two main focuses are developing Deeper Listening skills and properly formulating and deployment of questions. Clear out your preconceived ideas of coaching. Open your mind and heart to a transformed way of leadership.

Coaching can certainly take place outside the spiritual realm. However, if part of your coaching belief is to assist the coachee in a heart, mind, body, and soul transformation, your own spiritual preparation must first take priority. No amount of material, other physical resources, and equipping will be sufficient without spiritual preparation. Stop reading and take time right now to make a commitment to God for personal, spiritual preparation now and each time you enter into a coaching session for the rest of your life.

Prepare for a great journey and - May the turning of this page be the beginning of a greatly effective leadership lifestyle influencing the lives of many for generations to come.

Chapter One

Listening – Much More Than Using Your Ears

"Listening isn't that hard to do. What's difficult is making the decision to try." William Beausay II.

We have all heard the saying, "God gave us two ears and one mouth, so He must've expected us to listen twice as much as we speak." This saying likely came about due to one of the weaknesses we have in humanity.

This weakness I am speaking of is the mistaken belief that what we have to say is more important than what we have to hear. Let me say that again. One of the weaknesses of humanity is the mistaken belief that what I have to say is more important than what I have to hear. As a coach, we must strive to eliminate this weakness from our being. A coach is one who will listen intently and ask appropriate questions to guide the coachee toward a desired goal – set by the coachee, not the coach.

Many times a listener, leader, approached with a concern will shut off his/her hearing to prepare an answer without fully listening to the concern. While the other person is voicing her concern, we are planning our rebuttal. We allow one sentence

7

or one phrase, perhaps one word, to determine the basis for our response. Do you know someone like this? We have all been there, on both sides of the fence.

In fact, you have just read 208 words in the previous 3 paragraphs, and your thoughts have drifted away at least once. Something I have written in those paragraphs has caused you to momentarily drift away in your thinking. Hopefully, you were able to pull yourself back and reread what you had missed.

Here is a simple test. Have you ever been introduced to someone and tried to recall their name two minutes later, to no avail? If we do this with something as simple as a name, how much more likely are we to act this way regarding a decision or an opinion?

Can we learn not to shut down our hearing until the person speaking completely voices his concern? Yes, we can. But it takes practice – a lot of practice for many of us. For some reason, it seems almost inherent to begin producing our rebuttal while the other person is still speaking. The defying issue here is while our brains are fascinating operational devices, they cannot process incoming information while at the same time manufacturing a response. We cannot cognitively soak in and process all the incoming information at the same time as attempting to formulate a response.

Let's look at a biblical personality for a guideline. Jesus always listened patiently to what people had to say. Not until after they finished did he respond. He always responded to their words and their logic. Matthew 16:1-4 speaks of one encounter Jesus had with the Pharisees and Sadducees (religious leaders).

Then the Pharisees and Sadducees came, and testing Him asked that He would show them a sign from heaven. ² He answered and said to them, "When it is evening you say, 'It will be fair weather, for the sky is red'; ³ and in the morning, 'It will be foul weather today, for the sky is red and threatening.' Hypocrites! You know how to discern the face of the sky, but you cannot discern the signs of the times. ⁴ A wicked and adulterous generation seeks after a sign, and no sign shall be given to it except the sign of the prophet Jonah." And He left them and departed. Matthew 16:1-4 NKJV

The Pharisees and Sadducees were testing Jesus, trying to trip Him up in front of a public audience. Even though Jesus knew what they were doing, He let them finish their question before He answered. Notice, when He did answer, He did not answer their question. Jesus answered their motive using their own logic. The Pharisees and Sadducees could not answer Jesus and were left standing murmuring amongst themselves as Jesus walked away.

You might ask what this has to do with coaching. Well, I'm not suggesting you run your coaching clients away. Jesus' question to these men required the engagement of deeper thinking to these men and everyone listening. To answer would have required a admitting a needed change in their thinking. The religious leaders did not want to change. So they left. Your coachee must be willing to explore the possibilities of needed change and adjustment in his/her thinking and actions.

Matthew 21:23-27 is another great example of someone challenging Jesus' authority. He answered the same way. Using their motives and logic.

[23] Now when He came into the temple, the chief priests and the elders of the people confronted Him as He was teaching, and said, "By what authority are You doing these things? And who gave You this authority?"

[24] But Jesus answered and said to them, "I also will ask you one thing, which if you tell Me, I likewise will tell you by what authority I do these things: [25] The baptism of John—where was it from? From heaven or from men?"

And they reasoned among themselves, saying, "If we say, 'From heaven,' He will say to us, 'Why then did you not believe him?' [26] But if we say, 'From men,' we fear the multitude, for all count John as a prophet." [27] So they answered Jesus and said, "We do not know."

And He said to them, "Neither will I tell you by what authority I do these things.

Jesus is coaching His audience into a discovery learning experience. First, He listened to their every word of inquiry. Then He asked a true thought provoking question. Every question we ask, every word that we speak should help lead others to a more purpose filled life – God's designed purpose. We can only do this when we listen and understand the concern or situation being expressed. When a person discovers answers for himself, he will more likely discover and buy into the needed adjustments in his life.

Remember when James and John asked to be seated at Jesus' left and right hand when He would come into His glory (kingdom)? Jesus heard them out, completely, before giving His answer. Then, He answered them completely and in God's wisdom.

The four gospels record many other examples of Jesus' listening skills. In each case, you'll find that Jesus listened carefully, patiently to what was being asked or voiced before He answered. By listening He knew the intent and was able to respond skillfully and with God's wisdom.

Jesus had the power of insight to know what people were thinking and their motives. Yet, He always listened patiently before delivering a response. If Jesus felt it important to listen, should we not deem it important as well?

When we stop listening and shut down our hearing, we shut our brains off from receiving the incoming information. We do not hear what others are saying to us. When we do not hear a person completely, we run the risk of not responding in a way that will positively impact them for a better productive life.

It is important to hear someone out to completely understand their motives and intent for bringing a concern to you. When we will listen to a complete thought presented to us, and take a moment to digest all that was presented, our response will be delivered with more skill and the wisdom of God.

More than your ears alone.

So far, this chapter has focused on listening as we normally think of listening. With our ears. But this type of listening is only a superficial listening. When we only listen to someone's words, we often miss the intent, motive, and concern of the individual speaking. As a coach and leader, it is imperative that we go well beyond this superficial listening.

It is true, God has given us two ears to receive the audible presentations that surround us. However, when we listen only to the words of one speaking, we miss out on the majority of what is being communicated. Researchers tell us that the words we speak represent only seven percent (7%) of our communication. If this is true, then 93% of what you communicate is by other means, not your words. Think on this for a minute. Most people rely on the spoken word as the main communication from person to person. Yet, the spoken word is only seven one hundredths of what is communicated. Less than ten percent! Are we really missing out on 93% of what people are communicating to us?

In most cases, we're not missing all 93%. You'll see as you read ahead, that you actually pick up on some of the other communication. Let me give you an example. Let's look at the sentence: "Jane is wearing that blue dress." I placed no emotion in that sentence, so how did you read it? Is what Jane is wearing a good thing or a disturbing one? How do you respond if a coworker makes this statement to you?

To explore this a little further let's say the co-worker comes to you in almost a whisper but a sharp tone and with emphasis on the word "that" and makes the statement, "Jane is wearing that blue dress." Is there a difference in the way you receive the comment? Next, let us add another detail. As your co-worker approaches with furrowed brow, eyebrows raised and fists clenched at her side she exclaims, "Jane is wearing that blue dress."

This is only three pieces of detail that help us to understand what is being communicated in this example. When you first read the sentence, there was no emotion to give you an indication of whether the co-worker liked or disliked the dress. As you read it your thought processes had to rely on a work-related experience from your past with one of your co-workers. As I added detail, your mind was given more information to form your own picture of the scenario playing out.

This is how deeper listening plays out in your life every day. You will see that not only words spoken, but many other factors play a part in the information you receive each day. In every interaction, you find yourself in with another person or persons, the communication goes far deeper than your ears. In this and the ensuing chapters you will find out how to read and capture not only the seven percent of verbal communication, but much of the other 93 percent as well.

Listening – it is much more than using your ears.

Listening with five senses

Listening with all five senses almost sounds oxymoronic, doesn't it? If hearing is one of the five senses, how do you listen with taste, smell, and touch? When listening to someone speak, be it a social conversation or a formal work setting, all five senses are engaged. Why not employ them in the gathering of information to help us comprehend the speakers message? I do not want us to get bogged down with this, as there is much more intrinsic information to come in later chapters. For the moment let me give a brief paragraph or two on each of the five senses.

Hearing – of course this is the sense we normally relate to listening. And it gives us a receiver for all audible information around us. What I want to assist you in understanding is do not use your ears only for the intake of words. A person communicates with other audible information as well. In the chapter on body language you will read of voice tone and inflection, as well as other factors being communicated audibly.

13

Taste – While this is likely the least used of the senses for gathering information in a conversation, it can produce valuable information. The only application for the sense of taste is found in the mouth in the form of taste buds. These are found on your tongue and the roof of your mouth. No other place in or out of your mouth can you experience taste. While you are not always chewing or eating something to taste, your taste buds are always active. If you've ever been outside where there is a peculiar odor in the air, oftentimes you not only smell the stench, but your taste buds capture it as well. Whether coming from the speaker or not, the information gathered by your taste buds can attribute to your understanding of the information being conveyed by the speaker.

Smell – much like the sense of taste, smell may not be a primary source of learning and listening, but in certain situations can provide you with needed information. The smelling sensors of your nose pick up aromas, scents, and odors all around you. If the person speaking to you has not bathed in a while, you will know it. And the incessant odor will influence your listening and information gathering abilities. This one we understand, but the opposite is just as true.

I once wrote a course titled *Improving Your Job Seeking Skills.* Preparing for an interview, I instructed job seekers not to wear perfume, cologne, or after shaves to an interview. If you've ever been in closed quarters with someone who over did the perfume or after shave, you know what I am talking about. One, you do not know if the person you will be speaking with has allergies to those fragrances which will shut down his hearing. But, also, I showed in that job seeking course that in preparation for leaving your house you have already clothed yourself with up to 13 fragrances (soap, shampoo, laundry detergent, antiperspirant, hairspray or gel, toothpaste, etc.). Do you really need one more overpowering fragrance? Learn to use your nose to gather useful information for the situation.

Touch – Learning even the basics of touch and how touch relates to gathering information in a conversation (coaching situation) will assist you greatly. The sense of touch gives you an understanding of structure, surface, rigidity, resiliency, and consistency. If the person you are coaching has an object they want you to advise about, touching it will tell you if it is soft, coarse, thick, resilient, or other. This information assists you in the coaching process.

Not only objects, the sense of touch comes into play more often with the touch from a person or the touching of another person. Do you realize that if you are consoling a person there is a major difference in reception whether you touch him/her on the shoulder or the elbow? Which would you say would be more comforting to this person, a touch or pat on the back of the shoulder or a touch on the elbow? You likely thought shoulder. That is what we do in our culture, right? However, this is not true. A touch on the shoulder can seem condescending or superficial. Whereas a touch on the elbow or just above the elbow is more often construed as a helping hand – "we are going to get through this together."

Think of this analogy. If you were helping an elderly man across the street, would you place your hand on his back as if pushing him? Or would you place your hand under his arm at the elbow, or just above his elbow? The elbow suggests the helping hand. We'll learn more in the chapters on body language.

Sight – I saved this one for last because, it is in my opinion, the most critical sense we can use in understanding what is being communicated. Your eyes take in a great deal of information from your surroundings. We will devote an entire chapter to the eyes and how to use them in deeper listening as well as reading another person's eyes. If you are studying this for the first time perhaps you will be intrigued, amazed, and even overwhelmed by the amount of information that can be gathered by the eyes. You might even be stunned by how many times what your eyes and ears take in simultaneously are two totally different messages. Your eyes are perhaps your greatest God-given listening apparatus.

The words spoken and the eye contact, facial expressions, and body language of a person speaking are not always conveying the same message. Listening only to a person's words will most often not allow you to assess the reality of a situation. After all, Listening is much more than using your ears.

Chapter Two

Using Deeper Listening Skills

*"Hearing is an auditory process. Listening is an intentional process. "*Val Hastings

We all desire to have others listen to us but most people never attempt to develop listening skills. Our normal listening skills focus more on us than the other person. While the other person is speaking, we make a quick judgment then begin to formulate a response. Our response is based only on a fraction of the information shared and is based on our own experience.

While this may be in the nature of our culture, it is not the best practice. Great leaders and worthy coaches understand the importance of allowing a person to voice his thoughts entirely before responding. In fact, great leaders will often pause after the other person stops speaking. This can be a key to knowing someone is listening with deeper listening skills. If you have truly been listening to the entirety of the discourse, you will not have had time to prepare a response. Therefore, you cannot reply immediately. It is okay and prudent to take a few seconds to prepare your thoughts before replying in any situation.

Reflect on your own experiences. Do you remember a time when a friend or boss replied to something you said and your thoughts were, "You didn't hear what I said, did you?" We've all been there. Someone gives us their opinion or advice based on the first sentence or two we spoke, when we did not get into the meat of our query until sentence five. His advice or opinion did not have any bearing to our quest. Perhaps you also thought of a time when you may have answered too quickly. We've all been there as well.

Listening to all that is being said is critical in coaching. This is not an easy thing to do and is in fact a learned trait of great leaders and coaches. For every coach the discipline to carefully listen without interrupting with an answer, advice, or suggestion is a learned skill. It certainly does take practice. It is, perhaps, the most difficult trait to adhere to, like a golfer keeping his head down after striking the ball.

Listening to all that is being said is critical. But, not even this is using deeper listening skills. As mentioned in Chapter one, deeper listening involves much more than hearing the words being spoken. The human auditory system is the sensory structure for receiving all sounds. In other words, our ears pick up more than words. Our auditory system begins with our ears, but is made up of the corti, hair cells, neurons, tectorial membrane, nerve fibers and other parts that we'll not get into here. After all this is not a biology book.

However, there is one interesting tidbit I want to mention. There are two types of hair cells in your auditory system. Inner hair cells (with a six syllable technical name) actually transduce sound waves into electrical activity that nerve fibers transfer to the brain. The brain then, instantly searches our catalog of stored information to identify the sound.

Driving in your car you hear a blaring siren. What is the first thing you do? Your foot automatically backs off the accelerator and you begin looking all around to see where the siren is coming from. How did you know to do this? Stored information. Perhaps you were listening to the radio or driving in silence. Without warning the sound of the siren reached your ears and the auditory system took over. You were not listening for or expecting that sound. But your auditory system alerted you and possibly kept you from being involved in an accident or perhaps from a speeding ticket.

Your ears (and auditory system) pick up and transmit information to your brain all day long. Much of the information, like the siren, is information you were not looking for or expecting. A worthy coach learns to use the auditory system to gather valuable information for assisting the coachee.

Voice Inflection and Tone

Two of the intrinsic applications for the auditory system (other than gathering words) is voice inflection and tone. Both, voice inflection and tone are controlled by emotion. As a coach it is wise to learn to detect the emotion in a person's inflection and the tone of his/her voice.

Voice inflection is the variation of modulation in one's voice. It is the raising and lowering, the softness or hardness of a person's voice. Webster's Dictionary says the definition of inflection is: the act or result of bending. The modulation of one's voice consists of the cadence, variation, and pitch. As we speak these three things change due to emotional charges attached to the words we are sharing.

When leading coaching conferences I have participants partner up for an exercise to demonstrate voice inflection. One of the participants shares of a life experience as I call out certain topics. The other participant listens for voice inflections. I call out one topic and allow about 30 seconds before calling out a second topic. I repeat this for a third and sometimes a fourth topic. The topics vary but could include 1) a childhood disappointment, 2) seeing your bride walk down the aisle on your wedding day, 3) the tragic loss of a loved one.

Each of these will invoke certain emotions from each of us. As we speak about them our voice inflects due to the emotional attachment of the experience. Let's engage in a little experiment using a sentence from chapter one. You remember the sentence, "Jane is wearing that blue dress." Repeat this sentence three times using the information below.

First, you like it when Jane wears that blue dress. Say it (out loud) like you really like the way Jane looks in that blue dress.

"Jane is wearing that blue dress."

Second, you believe Jane is trying to work her way up the corporate ladder wearing clothing like that blue dress.

"Jane is wearing that blue dress."

Third, you realize that blue dress is the last gift Jane received from her mother before she passed away last year.

"Jane is wearing that blue dress."

The inflection of your voice changed with each rendering of that sentence. Why? Because of the emotional attachment you made due to the instructions given in each scenario. Not only inflection, my guess is your tone changed as well.

Listening to the tone of a person's voice will also give you information helpful for your coaching experience. A person's tone relates a specific style or manner of expression in speaking. The tone sets a specific pitch and vibration reflecting emotion. Most people consider one's tone of voice when that person is angry or mad. A worthy coach learns to recognize several other emotions attached to various voice tones as well; sadness, happy, excitement, surprise, discouragement, and fear.

The tone of any person's voice will vary according to emotions attached to the topic or experience being discussed. Notice the intentionality of the word "or" in the last sentence. A person's tone can vary due to either topic or experience. Example: A person speaking on the topic of losing a loved one will likely express sadness through her voice tone. Yet, a person who has lost a loved one within the last week, will likely express sadness in her tone on most any topic. Her sadness is related to a recent experience, not a topic. The first person may remember the sadness of grief. Thereby, rendering a voice tone of sadness. The second lady would be at that very moment experiencing grief, evidenced in her voice tone.

Try an exercise this week. As you interact with others, at home, work, organizations, or pursuits of pleasure, listen for the voice tones and inflections as others speak. How are their emotions being evidenced in their speech?

Open up a new world to your listening. Begin listening for emotion in voice tone and inflection as others speak. Don't worry about missing something being said. Before long you will be gathering information from voice tone and inflection without realizing you are doing it.

Open Minded Listening

As a coach, it is imperative that you keep an open mind. We have already mentioned to listen completely, without planning your response. In addition, we must strive to listen without judgment or our own agenda. The purpose of coaching is to assist the coachee in fulfilling his/her God-given purpose. Therefore, we must look and listen for God's agenda. Not ours or the coachee.

I believe every person has exactly what he needs to fulfill God's plan for his life. Unfortunately, most people never uncover or unearth what God has planted deep within to fulfill that purpose. As a coach, to assist someone in discovering parts of this gifting, brings a sense of pure joy. And it requires using deeper listening skills without an agenda.

As you listen for voice inflection and tones take note of how these correspond with the words being spoken. Listen for frustrations and motivations. People often share these without realizing the importance. When a person speaks of something he/she is passionate about, his/her voice tone will raise to a slightly higher pitch. Also, the cadence or speed of speech will increase. When voicing frustrations, a person's modulation often drops, and the emotion of sadness appears in their voice tone and facial expressions.

If we are listening with an agenda, we will miss these key communication factors. Too many times when someone is speaking to us with beliefs other than what we hold, we begin forming a judgment against his discourse. Unfortunately, this judgment is formed long before we hear the real objective. Listen to how the words relate to voice tones, inflection and body language (covered later in this book).

Someone has said, "Tell someone something long enough and they will believe it." I cannot tell you how many times I have found this to be true. Some people have been told something long enough that their words display belief, even if the belief is complete opposite of the facts. If a young woman has been told all her life that she will never amount to anything, it can take hold on her belief system. Listening for voice tone and inflection can aid you in determining how deep the belief is.

But repetition is not the only provider of wrong learning. One of the greatest lessons I've ever heard about is that of Jane Elliot, 3rd grade teacher in a small Iowa town. The day following Dr. Martin Luther King Jr's assassination in 1968, she tried an experiment that became an every year lesson and has been used in other schools, government, and prison settings. The lesson to be learned was about discrimination. She divided the class between blue eyed students and brown eyed. She proceeded to state that blue eyed students were smarter, better learners, better people and harder workers. She set parameters giving limitations to brown eyed students and privileges to blued eyed ones.

The brown eyed students were given special collars to wear to identify them from a distance. Mrs. Elliot says that within five minutes she watched a change taking place. Children who had studied and played together all their lives, became enemies almost instantly. Condescension set in and the brown eyed students withdrew and did poorly on their class studies. All because they were told they were not as smart or as good as blue eyed students.

The next day Mrs. Elliot stated she had it backwards. Brown eyed students were indeed the smarter students and better people than blue eyed. She reversed all of the restrictions and privileges. The brown eyed students had never moved so fast as they did in removing their collars and placing them on one of their blue eyed classmates.

At the end of the second day, she brought the class together and debriefed the entire exercise. She had the children speak of their feelings and beliefs. Decades later those students remember the valuable lesson they were taught. They made statements like, "We're like a family. It was terrible to be treated that way. All these years later we refuse to hurt one another, in any way."

There have been a couple of documentaries produced on this and at least one book written. While there are many lessons to be learned from Mrs. Elliot's experiment, one that I want you as a coach to grasp is how quickly one's perception of reality can change his/her entire belief system. We need to understand this from two angles. First, how we respond could have a lasting effect on this person's belief system. Make sure it is one that will lead to God's purpose being fulfilled. Enter every coaching session with an open mind and without judgment. The second is, as we listen we need to train ourselves to pick up on all the information being conveyed audibly – words, emotion, inflection, and tone. After all, our intent is to use deeper listening skills.

Chapter Three

The Eyes Have It

*"The soul, fortunately, has an interpreter - often an unconscious but still a faithful interpreter - in the eye. "*Jane Eyre

We speak about 100 words per minute, yet we have the capability to think at up to 800 words per minute. Where do you think those extra thought words go? Our brain is processing something. But what? At the same time that we are listening, our brain is processing a myriad of other audible sounds within ear shot. If we are close enough to hear it, our auditory system is processing it. Those sounds that we are not focused on, our brain is storing them in another part of our memory cache.

As we have mentioned in earlier chapters, the information we receive audibly is only a small portion of what is being communicated. The greatest receptors of what is being communicated is through our vision. Our eyes receive the majority of all that is communicated to us. Some coaches today perform much of their coaching over the phone. But the previous statement of our eyes reception, is the reason I prefer to coach in person. If not in person, my preference is through a video format.

While the well-trained ear of a coach can pick up better than average information through audible communication, there is no substitute for face to face, in person communication. Most people cannot read body language over the phone. The eyes of the coach and the coachee are important pieces of the communication process.

The Eyes of the Coach Communicate

As the eyes of the person being coached always communicate valuable information to you, your eyes are continually communicating to the coachee as well. We will learn much about what the eyes communicate and how to read that communication in this chapter. As you learn how to read what the eyes of others are telling you, think on the communication of your own eyes.

What your eyes and body language communicate, will play a considerable role in how others relate to you. While you may have the best interest of your coachee in mind, the communication of your eyes and body language could have an adverse effect on your coachee opening to you.

Always make good eye contact with your coachee. As you enter the presence of the coachee look her directly in the eye – eye to eye. As you begin the coaching session, be certain to make good eye contact. Throughout your time with the coachee (individual or group), maintain consistent eye contact. I used the word consistent instead of continuous, because it is not natural to maintain continual eye contact.

In their book *The definitive Book of Body Language*, Allen and Barbara Pease state, "When we talk we maintain 40 to 60 percent eye contact, with an average of 80 percent eye contact when listening."[i] As a coach building a good rapport with a coachee your eye contact should meet theirs 60 to 70 percent of the time. Your eye contact with a coachee will encourage and support their trust in your coaching efforts.

Our natural bent is to make eye contact for a few seconds, looking away briefly every 30-45 seconds. If someone's speaking is enthralling to you, your eye contact may remain for longer periods. If you are interviewing or coaching another person and that person never breaks eye contact, it is likely he is either on drugs or a serial killer. Continual eye contact is simply not in our DNA. But good eye contact is critical in communication. Good eye contact reveals trustworthiness for the listener and respect for the person speaking.

Eye Movement, Breaking Contact

There also is much being communicated when a person breaks eye contact, even if only for a brief few seconds. Learning these communication points will lead you strongly in understanding the primary message of what is being verbally spoken. Learning these will also assist you in understanding what you might be communicating as you break eye contact.

Breaking eye contact is natural as discussed above. What happens to the eyes when contact is broken can reveal a symphony of information for you, the coach. Over the course of fourteen years in the corporate world I conducted more than 5,000 job interviews. This is where I first began studying body language and eye contact. There were several interesting lessons learned during that period that I will share with you throughout this book.

One of those lessons dealing with breaking eye contact is an interviewee looking toward the exit. When the person you are coaching or interviewing is uncomfortable, it is common for that person to glance toward the exit door in the room. Not once, but every few seconds. Now this is a subconscious action, but for the interviewer, I often found it amusing, especially if I knew the person had a reason for being uncomfortable. Continual glancing toward the exit is a subconscious statement, "I do not want to be here." It is as if that person is planning his escape route.

In coaching, I want the coachee to unearth what he/she is uncomfortable about. This will be very beneficial in the coachee moving forward toward his goals and fulfilling his life purpose. A worthy coach will not in most cases expose the coachee's continual glance at the door, or other body language that may reveal the coachee's discomfort. Instead, a worthy coach will probe other areas of the conversation that might unearth the cause of discomfort.

In breaking eye contact, a person may look at various parts of the room. It is not always about planning an escape. Bright colors, light, windows, slight movement in drapes or papers caused by HVAC air circulation, an antique or particular piece of furniture or artifact. When in someone's office, I often look at books on a bookshelf as I break eye contact. Over the years, I've realized I am looking for familiar book titles, books that I've read and are on the shelves in my office. When people break eye contact they are doing the same. They are looking for items of familiarity, comfort, and safety.

The eyes also reveal other pertinent information as they break eye contact. Certain eye movements without gazing at a particular spot or area of the room reveal some of the greatest non-verbal information you can capture as a coach. Learning these will benefit you greatly. However, we must take caution not to rely on only one glance or gesture. In the chapter on body language we will speak about reading clusters. For now, let's look at eye glance direction.

Eye glance direction refers to the direction a person's eyes move as they break eye contact. These are interesting and can assist you as you learn to read eye movement in connection with body language. When a person is speaking or during a pause in speech there are seven general regions to which a person's eyes may move. Left, right, up and to the left, up and to the right, down to the left, down to the right, and down centered.

Horizontal Glances

Researchers believe a person's glance to the left or right reveals the difference between recall and fabrication or creation. We also have been taught that the left side of the brain uses recall, while the right side of the brain is the creative side. With this in mind let us look at what researchers tell us about eye movement.

When the eyes move horizontally to the left the person is using recall. When the eyes move horizontally to the right, the person is creating, building, or fabricating. Horizontal eye movement is believed to correspond to sound. In other words if you asked someone to sing Jingle bells, his eyes would likely shift left, recalling the sounds of Jingle Bells. If you asked that person to whistle a new tune, it is likely his eyes would shift to the right while fabricating a tune.

Upward Glance

What about upward glances? When a person speaking glances upward and to the left, again they are likely using recall. Recall helps us to bring to the forefront of thinking the stored facts and memories in our brain. When a person is looking up and to the left, she is likely recalling the situation or circumstances from memory. On the other hand if her glance is up and to the right, she is likely trying to create or recreate the incident or situation.

This is interesting to observe. Though some have said eyes moving up and right is a signal of lying, we must be careful not to make those assumptions without knowing the facts and taking into consideration a cluster of communication signals. While this could be an indicator of fabricating a lie, it is not the only explanation. A traumatic event can cause a person to bury or discard memories. It is not uncommon for people to shift to a construction or fabrication mode, trying to piece together the events. The essential key for the coach comes in determining when someone is fabricating a story or piecing it together with the known and unknown facts. Upward left is recall, upward right is fabrication.

Downward Gaze

While the horizontal and upward glances take on two differing positions, the downward glance can take on elements of three differing positions. As the horizontal glance relates to auditory, and upward glances toward the recall or fabrication of imagery, downward glances reflect feelings and introspection. Glancing or staring at the floor when speaking demonstrates personal internal feelings related to what is being said.

In years past the thought was, if someone looks at the floor and cannot look you in the eye when they are speaking, they are telling a lie. We must be cautious, not to jump to conclusions. It is possible that the person is lying, but there are several other possibilities as well. Just as looking up to the right is a sign of fabrication, yet not always fabricating a lie, so it is with looking down.

I was asked to sit in on a second interview of a pastoral candidate with a pastor search committee. There were some not necessarily red flags, but uncertainties in the minds of the search committee members. I was asked to observe the body language of the candidate as the committee interviewed. Everything was going fine until a particular subject was brought up. Immediately, the man's head tilted down and his vision pointed to the floor about three feet in front of his feet. His gaze remained there until he finished his response.

About five minutes later he was asked another question about the same situation. Once again, immediately, his head dropped and his gaze was on the same spot on the floor. This happened three times during the interview. Throughout most of the near hour and a half interview his eye contact was good, his body language was relaxed and normal. His voice tones and inflection were fine. So, why at this one subject did things seem to unravel for this pastor?

What I told the committee afterwards was, he showed no signs of fabrication or lying. Nor did his eye contact or body language show signs of disbelief in his own words (which does happen often in interviews). What his cluster of body language was demonstrating was shame. His loss of eye contact and body language were telling me that this was a man who had something happen to him at an earlier church pastorate that still brought shame to his mind. It was not something that had been of his doing. Rather it was something done by others on his watch as pastor. His eyes gave verification to what had been told to the committee by outsiders who knew of the situation. - sidenote: The committee recommended him and the church called him to be their pastor.

When eye contact is broken and the speaker is looking down at the floor two to four feet in front of their shoes this is a demonstration of internal emotion. She is speaking on a subject that brings internal feelings of shame, disappointment, inferiority, disbelief, or guilt. Researchers believe looking down and to the right is a stronger display of the kinesthetic (getting in touch with something about self), while down and left is leaning toward an internal dialog (someone talking to themselves).

In my study of body language there is a third concept of the downward gaze, straight down in front of the person's feet (from four inches to four feet. I was sitting in the office of another consultant/coach one morning as he was describing some of the events of a meeting he had been in the previous evening. He had been asked to attend to help the church leaders clarify an issue.

He began telling me of the pastor's delivery of information that other leaders were skeptical and wary of. When he finished I stated: "Let me tell you what he (the pastor) was doing as he spoke." I sat up on the edge of the couch and said, "He looked down at the floor about six inches in front of the toes of his shoes." Making a similar motion, looking down, with my hands and knees, I continued. "His knees were rapidly moving in and out as if they were going hit and back out again. And he kept this up the whole time he was speaking, never looking up, didn't he?"

My host for the morning, looked at me with wide eyed surprise, and said, "How did you know that? That's exactly what he did."

I knew the pastor and had sat in his office before. I replied to my host, "That is a nervous compulsion that he cannot control. It happens every time he shares what he knows to be an untruth or a deceitful pretense." His eye movement was the first indicator. The knee movement was simply an involuntary reaction to what was going on in his heart.

I have sat in several meetings like this. Meetings when people are sharing one thing with their words, yet their eye contact and body language is screaming something totally different. There are times when I wish I could video some of these because they are textbook examples of communication far greater and differing from their spoken words. A person's eyes are the most telling of all communication.

There is so much more the eyes communicate. Let me close out this chapter with a couple of these. First, the pupils of the eye are fascinating in what they communicate. You're not likely to be able to focus on a person's pupils in a coaching session, but knowing this may give you valuable insight. We know that the pupil dilates according to light. But, did you know the human eye also dilates and contracts according to emotion and mood swings? When a person gets excited his pupils can dilate up to four times the normal. Men, if you do not believe me try this at home. Look into your wife's eyes. Then scare her and look again to see the size of her pupils. Okay, maybe that's not a good idea. Perhaps, do some other research on it. Likewise, when a person experiences a negative mood swing his/her pupils will contract and appear smaller. Any words, images, or actions that stimulates the brain will cause the pupils to increase in size.

One other eye communication revealer is blinking. This is one you can easily observe. A sudden increase in blinking is normally a sign of anxiety and deceit. A great exhibition of this was evidenced in a recent presidential debate by one particular candidate. It was so evident I pointed out to my wife who has not studied these traits. Each time a subject was broached about something this candidate was being scrutinized for, her eye blinking increased dramatically.

Researchers have related sudden increased eye blinking with anxiety and feeling for a necessity of crafting or fabricating a response, hiding or withholding information. While I pointed out one politician, others have been observed with the same increased blinking. Watch your news casts and interviews with politicians and industry leaders. Rapid eye blinking is an involuntary reaction – and one that would be extremely difficult to train away.

The eyes have so much to reveal to us. We will learn in the facial expressions chapter how the eyes change with certain universal expressions. With surprise, a person's eyes will always widen, no matter what culture or part of the world they live in. Anger always brings a glare to the eyes. As coaches and leaders, it is imperative to be a continual learner, studying the amazing communication from the eyes. After all, the eyes are the revealing interpreter of the soul.

Chapter Four

What's in a Face?

"Few realize how loud their expressions really are. Be kind with what you wordlessly say." Richelle E. Goodrich

What is in a face? Does a face really lend to the communication of conversation? Yes, certainly. Next to the eyes, facial expressions may reveal more than any other part of the body when it comes to communication. The fact is, your face is continuously communicating something about what you are thinking, feeling, or saying. Even when you are not talking. According to researchers, even when you sleep.

Learning to make and maintain good eye contact, will reveal to you much more than what the eyes communicate. While you are making eye contact, your peripheral vision will capture evidences of communication from other areas of the head and face. Some of these are involuntary. Even with training, politicians (and others) cannot hide all of these. The brain controls the facial muscles and you cannot shut these off or control them. Actually, learning what these are and watching politicians can be fun. Their words may say one thing while their facial expressions are speaking very clearly, the opposite. And it's not only politicians. Observing these in everyday conversations and interviews can be quite revealing and entertaining.

Universal Facial Expressions

There are certain facial expressions that are universal. No matter where your travels take you, what the language or living habitat, these seven expressions relate the same emotions and feelings. It matters not whether you were raised and live in wealth or poverty, inner city, suburban, or rural, a nation of affluence or a third world country, these expressions convey the same emotions. These seven basic emotions are disgust, surprise, contempt, happiness, anger, sadness, and fear. I encourage you to read some of the research on these basic seven. But for now, let me give you a brief explanation how each one is demonstrated in facial expressions.

Disgust is defined as a marked aversion aroused by something highly distasteful. Disgust conveys repugnance. Disgust is revealed in facial expressions with a wrinkling of the nose. The level of disgust will determine the degree of wrinkling. A wrinkling of the nose gives the appearance of the eyebrows drawing together. Also, the upper lip is raised or elevated from its normal dormant position.

The expression of disgust may appear in different regions of the world by various thoughts or ideas based on the living practices of the person or people group. I have eaten calamari (squid) and enjoyed it. However, I have never considered eating a live squid as I watched travelers to another land eat on a recent television show. Even typing that statement likely brought an expression of disgust to my face. The facial expression is the same around the globe while based on our own level of accepted behavior.

Surprise brings three immediate changes to the face no matter where you live or how tough you consider yourself to be. With the element of surprise, the eyebrows raise, eyes widen, and the mouth opens. Remember, these are involuntary actions. This is why you might hear someone say, "Her eyes got as big as saucers." The mouth opening is not always a gaping, dropping of the jaw. Many times, it is a small opening between the lips. For those who normally keep their lips together, it could be only a slight breach between the lips. No matter the width of mouth opening, it will be accompanied by the eyes widening and raised eyebrows.

One thing to remember, while these expressions are involuntary (a person cannot help but make them), they are also brief in most scenarios. The element of surprise, for instance, lasts less than a second. If the person you are observing keeps the element of surprise expression on his face for longer, say three to four seconds, he is faking it. Because they are so brief, they are sometimes referred to as micro expressions. You may not catch them all. However, it is important to know them, for the ones you do observe will be of benefit to you as you help your coachee move forward.

Example: You are speaking with a coachee or employee and you bring up a topic which you know this person should not know the details. His eyes widen, eyebrows raise, and his mouth gapes open a little wider than normal. If he maintains this look of surprise and perhaps even begins to verbally express his thoughts, regardless of what his words are saying, he knows more than he is letting on. You can then formulate your next question based not only on his words, but his facial expressions.

The same is true in a reverse scenario. If you broach a topic you believe the person to know about, yet she expresses the element of surprise (briefly), she very likely is hearing this for the very first time. The three quick, brief facial changes that always accompany the element of surprise, the eyebrows raise, eyes widen, and the mouth opens.

Contempt is the contemplative disapproval or dislike of some person or thing. Contempt appears in facial expression as one side of the upper lip is tightened and slightly raised. The tightening of the lip causes the cheek muscles on the same side to contract as well. Though the cheek muscles tightening is almost undetectable in most cases, the tightening and raising of

37

the lip, on one side only, is noticeable. This lip movement is usually not held long. It is brief and will appear more noticeable on some people more than others.

Contempt is an emotional response toward a person or thing that we internally determine is beneath our dignity and unworthy of our attention, respect, or concern. This determination is revealed as an expression of low regard for the object or person held in contempt. Contempt always reveals itself with a negative connotation. A person revealing contempt might express her thoughts to others in hopes they will address the contemptible. However, she is not likely to confront the person or item of contempt, but, rather alienate the contemptible.

As a coach, recognizing the expression of contempt can assist in leading the coachee in realizing and addressing the underlying issues concerning the contempt. Contempt can hold a person back from becoming his/her best. Until the cause of the feeling of contempt is addressed, a person cannot reach his/her greatest potential.

Happiness is revealed in facial expressions with upward pushed cheeks. As the cheek muscles push upward both corners of the mouth are pulled upward as well. Another effect of the cheek muscles pushing upward is noticed around the eyes. As the cheek muscles push up, the muscles around the eyes contract exposing the appearance of crow's feet or wrinkles around the outer edges of the eyes.

Happiness is considered a mental or emotional state of well-being defined by positive or pleasant emotions. Happiness is almost always an outward expression of satisfaction with one's life. While a person may not be satisfied with every aspect of his life, when thinking or speaking on the areas he is pleased with, facial expressions will exhibit happiness. Reading happiness in a coachee's expression is a great doorway for a coach to assist the coachee in finding the paths of passion and skill. Upward pushed cheeks, raised corners of the mouth, and the appearance of crow's feet or wrinkles are all communicators of happiness.

Anger is not necessarily the opposite of happiness. However, the two cannot simultaneously exist about the same thought. Things of pleasure bring about happiness, and anger is considered a strong feeling of displeasure and usually of resentment. Anger is exhibited in facial expression by the eyebrows drawing down over the eyes and appear to be drawn closer together. At the same time the eyes glare. The lips appear to narrow left to right and if only for a brief second the lips will close.

According to R. DiGiuseppe and R. Tafrate in Understanding Anger Disorders, "Anger is used as a protective mechanism of the body to cover up fear, hurt or sadness. Anger becomes the predominant feeling behaviorally, cognitively, and physiologically when a person makes the conscious choice to take action to immediately stop the threatening behavior of another outside force."[ii]

Reading anger in your coachee assists in identifying and strategically planning to avert and move beyond destructive behaviors. As long as anger persists in one area, a person cannot fully function in improving his/her disposition in other areas of life. Addressing the causes, not the symptoms, of anger is essential in making forward progress toward our greatest potential. Facial expressions of anger are exhibited by the eyebrows drawing down over the eyes and drawing closer together while the eyes exhibit a glaring effect.

Sadness is recognized fairly easy. You likely learned to identify sadness at an early age. Sadness is characterized as an emotional pain associated with, feelings of disadvantage, loss, despair, grief, helplessness, disappointment and sorrow. An individual experiencing *sadness* may become quiet or lethargic, and withdraw themselves from others.

The emotion of sadness appears in facial expression through a drooping of the upper eyelides. This may be slight and undetectable. But along with this appears a loss of focus in the eyes. The lips correspond with a slight turning down. Other muscle movement you might notice include a tensing of the chin directly below the lower lip, and a puffed out lower lip. Sadness can also produce a loss of eye contact.

It is imperative for a coach to assist the coachee in identifying a course for reversing or moving through a sad state of emotion. This approach must be done gently. The first step is to guide the coachee to identify the cause of the sadness. Identifying the cause will allow the coach to formulate questions to bring the coachee to her own determinations for a course of action. Never give the answer. Always ask questions that will lead the coachee to discover the applicable answer. (We'll discuss more about this in later chapters.)

Fear is the unpleasant, often strong emotion caused by anticipation or awareness of danger. When our brains receive signals of possible impending danger from any part of the body, it will activate impulses through the neurons of our nervous system. The result of these actions traveling to different nerve endings cause muscle reactions. The facial expressions resulted from these warnings include; raised eyebrows pulled toward center, raised upper eye lids, tense lower eyelids, and lips lightly stretched horizontally often accompanied by an almost gritting of the teeth.

An interesting note is that while each set of muscles is acting independently of the others, every group is acting simultaneously to produce a cluster of reaction. You have seen this cluster on faces before. Perhaps you recognized it as fear. It is possible that seeing this in someone you were speaking with, you also reacted similarly. Example: You are standing on a golf course with a buddy and someone yells "Fore". If the person beside you suddenly shows the elements of fear, it is likely that you will exhibit some of these as well.

Have you ever been in a theatre watching a movie full of suspense, when one of the actors startlingly exemplifies fear? If the director did a good job building the suspense, many people watching the movie will also demonstrate fear in their facial expressions. Sitting in a movie theatre when this happens, can be an amusing experience – if you knew it was about to happen.

A person can experience fear simply by speaking about a subject that brings him fear. As a coach, you can witness his trepidation of fear in his facial expressions. When you see this, it is time to help him unpack his fear. The improper way is, "Tell me what scares you or brings fear to you?" The best way is to allow the coachee to enter this area of fear through a side-door of the psyche. You'll read about how to do this in the chapters on questions later in this book.

These seven basic emotions cause the involuntary muscle reactions related for each one. The facial expressions as listed above are only a portion of the communication being sent. It is a vital part of the communication. There are other facial expressions that communicate as well. Flaring of the nostrils, a furrowed brow. There is a difference between a person cocking her head to the left as opposed to the right. Hint: the eyes up left and up right have a direct correlation.

Portions of people's faces turn red for differing reasons. Ear lobes turning red communicate something different than red cheeks. Ears turning red is often from nervousness. Cheeks turning red in conversation is most commonly associated with embarrassment. Some people's mouths are naturally turned downward on the ends. Does this mean this person is always sad? Of course not.

I trust you are beginning to see the idea and importance of reading clusters of communication signals. Facial expressions communicate a lot of information and combined with other communication factors will help you evaluate a complete communication package.

After all, few of us realize how loud our expressions really are. Be kind with what you say with your face.

Chapter Five

Body Talk – Upper Body

" Where body language conflicts with the words that are being said, the body language will usually be the more 'truthful' in the sense of revealing true feelings." Glen Wilson

Body Talk. Is that an oxymoron? Bodies don't talk, do they? Bodies may not talk in a verbal language. However, they do speak a language all their own – loud and clear, if you know what to watch for. While it is uncertain how long body language has been studied, we know it has been used to communicate since the earliest records of man. As mentioned in chapter one, Jesus used it during His years on earth. We know body language has been a research topic for nearly a century. Ray Birdwhistell is credited with pioneering the study of nonverbal communication among humans. Birdwhistell estimated that we have 250,000 facial expressions. Aren't you glad we did not attempt to disclose all 250,000 in the last chapter.

Not only facial expressions Birdwhistell and others have provided us with great tools in reading and understanding what the body is communicating. We have already looked at the audible, vision, and facial expressions. Moving on down the body, what other parts are involved in communication? The head itself is one, then the shoulders, arms, torso, legs, and hands. If it is capable of moving and responding to the brain, it is likely to give off communication indicators.

In these next two chapters, we will deal with some of the major communicating body parts that are of great assistance to the coach in reading the complete communication package. This is not in any way to be considered a complete and exhaustive study of how the body in general or the parts in particular communicate. Rather, it is to you as a coach and leader additional tools to assess a situation and assist in helping the individual or organization forward to being more productive and effective.

Reading Clusters

If you have ever heard anyone speak on body language, likely the first item you learned or remember is that a person sitting with arms folded across his chest is bored or uninterested. If you've been taught this, you can scratch it from your memory. While this is one possibility, it is not always true, especially in our western (hemisphere) culture. People sit with their arms folded for several reasons. For men, it is one of many security or protection signals we communicate. It can also be a contemplative signal. For others, folding of the arms is simply trying to keep warm.

To understand what the folded arms are communicating, you must learn to read other body language signals as well. When you can put two or more simultaneous gestures together, you are on track to understanding a communication signal (communicator). The more gestures that are aligning with a particular emotion or feeling, the greater the communication. The greater the communication signals, the easier it is to read and understand how the person feels and what she believes about the subject at hand. The more you can understand, the better equipped you will be to help the individual or organization.

A man sitting with his arms folded across his chest with eyes glazed over (as looking into a distant land) is probably bored or uninterested in your topic. However, the man sitting next to him might also have his arms folded across his chest and his gaze is not at you but upward and to the right. Remember from chapter three this is a reflective, retrieval signal. You have said something that has this man using his memory recall to substantiate his desire to believe and follow through with what you have stated.

A woman sitting with her arms folded, hands tucked between arm and side, may be cold. Look for other signals as legs crossed and pulled back under her chair, shoulders raised as if protecting or warming the neck, tenseness in extremities, shoulders, and neck. Perhaps you didn't realize the body, while sitting in a meeting, could give so many evidences of cold. And I didn't even mention a red nose or shivering body. This is reading a cluster to gain a more accurate estimate of what is being communicated.

Learning to read clusters in body language is not only beneficial to understand what is being communicated. It also makes you a much better listener. People, coachees especially, will appreciate you more and will be more open to share with you what you need to hear to assist them in reaching their greatest potential. The remainder of this chapter will deal with individual gestures. It is important to learn them individually, so that you will be able to identify them in clusters for a greater understanding of what is being communicated.

Shoulders

While we do not think of the shoulders as having much movement, they are communicators. Shoulders can pull upward, lower downward, round themselves inward, and pull backward. Each of these motions communicate something about the emotions and feelings of the person. Most of these are unintentional. Shoulder movement often happens involuntarily.

We recognize shoulders raised momentarily as a shrug. What do you think of when a person shrugs his shoulders?... A shrug is a common expression when someone is communicating, "I don't know." But how can you know this is what is being communicated with a shrug? Look for a cluster – multiple body part signals implying, "I don't know?" Parts of a cluster in this scenario could be; raised eyebrows, arms down to one's side with palms facing forward.

However, a shrug can also be a person's communicator for, concealment "I don't want to share." Other cluster indicators for this could include, lowered eyebrows drawn together, quick slight raising of the corners of the mouth, and palms turned down, facing backward or hidden behind the back.

Shoulders that move forward in a rounding inward motion is normally associated with a person subconsciously trying to make themselves appear smaller, unseen. When pulled up and back the subconscious is wanting to appear larger. This can be a defensive indicator. Body communicators like this are spontaneous displays of superiority, while the inturning of shoulders (to appear smaller) are subconscious reactions of inferiority, submission, or not wanting to be noticed.

If a person is speaking with you and you notice the shoulders turn to one side, it is an indicator the subconscious is desiring to make an exit. At a party, you may see a person's shoulders turn toward the food or drink table. This person's subconscious is desirous of refreshing her drink or partake of more appetizers. At other times, you might notice the shoulders turn toward the exit or a window. In either case, she is ready to leave your conversation. In each of these scenarios, the shoulders and feet will likely be pointing in the same direction.

Arms and Hands

Other than folded across the chest, what else can arms communicate? We have read how the eyes and facial expressions are two of the largest communicators of the human body. The arms and hands are, perhaps, the next greatest communicators. The arms are a continuation of the shoulders.

Shoulder movement will most often cause arm movement as well. Since the arms are an extension of the shoulders, they will move accordingly with the feeling or emotion causing the shoulder movement.

Arm placement can demonstrate defense, security, self-confidence, denial, and subservience or submission. Most often, arm movement will not by itself give a communication indicator. While placement of the arms can be one in a group or cluster of indicators, the arm itself is not a reliable communicator. To properly read the communication of the arms, you must observe the communication of the shoulders and hands. The hands are one of the greatest communicators for involuntary signals from the body.

I mentioned in an earlier exercise palms forward and backward. An open palm, faced up or forward conveys openness. When someone has something to conceal, even if it is thought or belief, his palms will not be visible. An act of concealment. When standing and conversing a person's hands are most of the time down at his side. If the palms are facing forward or in toward his leg (natural), this is considered an open palm. This shows openness and comfort with his immediate surroundings including the conversation.

The natural position of the hands will be slightly turned backwards, actually open to the thigh. Concealment is displayed when hands are completely turned with palms facing backward or hands behind the back. In an interview or a first coaching session a person may enter the room very tense. Her hands will be at her side with palms in or turned backward. As she begins to open up, you will notice her palms begin to turn or open up toward the interviewer or coach.

If a person's hands turn palms pointing backward while standing, it is likely, something is being concealed. However, before making that assumption, check for a cluster of communicators. It may simply be his beliefs are different than others in the conversation. Or, it is possible, he is concealing something more intrusive. This is a subconscious movement and can accompany other communicators forming a cluster relaying fear, contempt, dishonesty, sadness, or disengagement. Other forms of palm gestures revealing concealment include, closed hands, placing hands under his thighs while seated, and hands behind back while standing and speaking. Perhaps this is a carryover from childhood. Children often when lying or attempting to conceal something will often hide their hands behind their back – though the hands are empty. Hands behind the back can also be a sign of openness, rather than securing the frontal mid-section. Another reason to learn to read clusters.

One other concealment technique is hands in pockets. Men are more likely to carry their hands inside pockets. This is often a communicator that he is not interested in joining the conversation. Women are more open to conversation. Therefore, you seldom see women with hands in pockets (except to keep her hands warm).

When speaking, many people use hand movements to help convey their message. Have you ever heard, "She can't talk without using her hands." Or "Tie his hands and he can't speak."? I often use hand movements as I speak. Most of the time those hand movements are involuntary. But they are communicating. If a person speaking – especially speaking to a large group - uses a hand gesture, take note of the position of his palms. Are they facing up or down? A speaker's palms pointing up is a sign of welcome openness. It is an invitation. Palms pointing down however, is expressing dominance and control. He feels the need or compulsion to control.

Not only are these part of the subconscious of the speaker, they also create responses from the subconscious in the listener. Research has shown when the same speech or talk is given using a palms up approach to one group and a palms down approach to the second group, people from the first group are more receptive to the speaker and his talk. Not only are they more open, they also remember more from the talk and carry a more positive attitude out of the meeting. Those in the second group remembered little from the talk and had considerable less respect for or desire to hear the speaker again. Keep your palms open and facing upward or out to your coachee/audience.

One other hand gesture used in speaking that needs to be noted is pointing. Pointing a finger at a person or group is always received with a negative vibe. Pointing says, "I'm dominate, you're subordinate. You will do what I say." It is not always intended this way, but this is the perception. One theory is the pointing finger is actually a closed fist with the one pointing finger representing a club, as if relating back to caveman days. The pointing finger is one of the most annoying communicators anyone can use. Aside from annoying, it also draws the listener's attention away from the spoken words to judgment of the speaker. The pointing finger should be avoided at all costs in speaking, coaching, and leading. Even in giving direction it is better to use the open palm all fingers straight or slightly bent, in a panning motion.

Since my hands are often in motion when I speak, I have attempted to train myself to maintain an open hand facing outward or upward. To exaggerate the open friendliness, I also almost always keep my fingers open or separated from each other. Fingers pressed against each other signals a closed off security, Don't try to get close to me." Space between fingers displays openness, as if saying, "I'm approachable."

The Handshake

The hand and arm are also communicators during a handshake. In many areas of the business world one of the first teachings is a proper handshake. We are taught our handshake should be with a firm grip. However, to teach only to have a firm grip is poor teaching and falls short of the needed learning. It would be equivalent to an elementary school teacher teaching students how to write simple equations without ever teaching them how to solve those equations. 2+2= __.

Have you ever had someone's "firm" grip hurt you or cause your ring to cut into your fingers? I have had more than one woman share of being cut by their own ring, due to the forceful grip of a man's handshake. What would be the lasting impression of these women on the man who caused this unfortunate displeasure? These women resent and avoid the men who created this unpleasant experience – even if it was from her boss.

A firm grip is important, but a forceful pain-filled grip causes distrust and avoidance. It also, in the mind of the recipient, raises the question, "What is he overcompensating for?" This is where the distrust comes in. I once coached a pastor who was short in stature. I'm only five foot seven, and he was several inches shorter than me. From the very first time I met him it was easy to recognize this. We approached each other, his right arm cocked at the elbow, hand slightly in front of his hip. As we drew near I pulled my hand up to shake, his hand came at mine with the force of a truck and a movement that started from his torso, to his shoulder, and through his arm. Our hands met in an almost explosive clap and his fingers clamped down on mine like a vise. Each time we were together, I was greeted with this handshake for the next couple of months.

As one who reads body language and a coach, I realized this was simply his way of stating, "I'm not as small as I appear." And truly he was a giant of a man. A great pastor with a heart after God's own desires. Yet, subconsciously, he felt the need to over compensate. About five months into our coaching experience, I noticed his handshake was not as forceful. I'm not certain if it was only with me or if it had become less of an issue as we had worked on other areas of leading his congregation.

A firm grip is important, and your grip should always take into consideration the person you are about to shake with. You do not shake a woman's hand with the same grip or power you do a man. Men and women also approach a handshake differently. Most generally, men will approach a handshake with the palm slightly facing down as if to come in over the top of the other person's hand. This downward facing of the palm is a sign of dominance. The greater the angle from a 90-degree palm entering a handshake, the greater dominance is being displayed. It is part of the Alpha male in all men in western culture. Watch diplomats and politicians as they shake one another's hands.

Women on the other hand, in most cases will approach a handshake with the palm open, facing up at about a 30-45 degree angle. This is a sign of submission and respect for the other person. It is not a sign of weakness. It again demonstrates the openness and submission of women to be polite and courteous. The next opportunity that you have, perhaps in church this Sunday, shake hands with as many people as possible and observe the difference in handshakes between men and women. Take note of the position of the hand approaching, of dominance, and grip.

Hands and the Face

One other communicator of the hands to briefly touch on (no pun intended) is the hands on the face of a listener. This will occur mainly when a person is seated, but can be witnessed in a standing position at times too. When a person listening has one or two fingers resting on his cheek, pointing upward, this is a sign of interest. This person's fingers are pointing to the mind, as if directing the words to contemplative thought. The speaker has this person's attention and cognitive resources. In almost all scenarios where the one or two forward fingers on the hand are resting on the cheek pointing upward, the thumb is generally under the chin. The thumb is not supporting the chin, only resting there.

A similar position is when the fore finger or two are resting over the upper lip or in front of the mouth rather than pointing upward. This person is listening, but reserved, not ready to make a judgment or response to what is being spoken. The finger(s) in front of mouth or upper lip is signifying, "I am listening, but not certain I agree yet." It is as if he is blocking or guarding his mouth from speaking. As he becomes convinced or satisfied, you will see the fingers move, often to the pointed up position described in the previous paragraph.

There is one other seemingly similar hand to face gesture that needs to be noted. This is when the fingers and thumb are in contact with the same areas of the face (pointing upward or over the lip, with one key difference. In the above communicators, the fingers and thumb are resting in the said positions. In this gesture, the opposite is observed. The head and face are resting on the fingers and thumb. In this communicator, it will appear that the head is being propped up by the hand and fingers. This person has lost interest and may fall asleep on you very soon. Well, they have at least lost interest and the speaker is not getting through. When you see this happening it is time to shift gears or take a break. Remember, fingers resting on face signals interest and listening. Head resting on fingers/hand signals disinterest and boredom.

The shoulders, arms, hands, fingers, & thumbs are such mammoth communicators. There is not enough space on these pages to cover it. What I have written can assist you in being a worthy, effective coach. After all, the shoulders, arms, and hands, produce body language usually more 'truthful' than words, in the sense of revealing true feelings and beliefs.

Chapter Six

Body Talk – Posture and Lower Body

"Your brain may do the thinking, but your legs move you to action." George Yates

In this chapter, we will continue our study of body language with an emphasis on posture and lower body extremities, legs and feet. While your posture, legs and feet are not as actively moving as the eyes, face, hands, and other upper body components, they are actively involved in communication.

Posture

As children most of us received speeches and words of caution about good posture. Though we might not have been concerned with them at the time, most of what we heard was good advice. Posture is important to our muscular and bone health later in life as well as our listening and learning abilities. Slouching posture truly does reduce the learning receptors of our body.

Whether standing or sitting, our posture is communicating to those around us. In my years of conducting more than 5,000 interviews with job applicants, posture during an interview became one of my telltale signs for a person's character. Most people enter an interview with a sense of nervousness. Therefore, the interview begins with him sitting in a pretty straight up, healthy postured position. As the interview progresses, the interviewee will begin to relax. For some this relaxing turns into a slouching position.

Slouching posture demonstrates little interest for the job or topic as well as a sign of disrespect. This disrespect may be concerning the interviewer and his company. It could be about work in general, or a disrespect for the work entailed. While slouching posture during an interview may not always be the only reason not to hire, it is a large communication indicator of the person's character. In my experience, slouching posture was one of a cluster of communicators – and it nearly always proved correct.

Conversely, straight up, healthy posture reflects interest in the job and the topic at hand. Yet, that was not always enough for me in an interview. Nerves could also keep a person sitting up straight in the chair. In most cases, I was seeking the person who would sit on the edge of his/her seat, leaning forward as we discussed the position being considered. Sitting on the front portion of the seat and leaning forward relays not only interest, but also intrigue and enthusiasm for the topic being discussed. As a coach, you should not only learn to watch for these types of posture, you should observe and have others observe your posture as well. Practice good healthy and enthusiastic posture.

In one church as I began serving as Transitional Interim Pastor, the staff suggested we do something to help the congregation to get to know me better. We settled on a Sunday evening interview process – "Get to know your pastor". I agreed and stated that I wanted all ministry staff members seated at the front of the auditorium with me. I had at least two reasons in mind: 1) it would give an appearance of the solidarity we shared (and we truly did). 2) This would relay a team effort and I could easily refer to or recognize team leaders as I answered questions and gave testimony.

As we discussed this special service, one staff member suggested we move enough wing back chairs from offices to sit in on the platform. My response was that would likely give off a wrong air about who we are and what I believed we should communicate. I feared people would envision his suggestion as seen on some Television evangelist programs with fancy high back chairs, where the hosts ask for money from those watching. While we were not going to be asking for money, perception in the mind of the listener is his reality.

My suggestion was that we not use wing back chairs. In fact, I did not want to use chairs at all. Instead, in the middle of the staff meeting I pulled out a tall counter stool, with no back, one like musicians sometimes use. I sat on it and inquired of the staff what they saw regarding my posture. Before they answered I asked the chairman of Deacons (who I invited to all our staff meetings) to share what he had observed about our posture while sitting in various chairs (including a couple wingbacks). People began straightening up in their chairs before he could speak. Most had retreated into a relaxed and even slouching position.

When asked what they observed in my posture on the stool, one foot on a rung of the stool and one foot on the floor, the replies included, "You're sitting straight."

"You're not slouching like us." Said a second staff member.

"No, he's not sitting straight." Stated a third. "He's actually leaning forward a little."

That last reply was the response I was looking for. I went on to explain the concept of seated posture and leaning forward as you read above. The following Sunday evening we conducted a well attended special service "Getting to Know Your Pastor" where any question could be asked of me – or the staff - from any person in attendance. We all sat on stools, not on the platform, but on the floor, the same level as our congregation. The following Monday at our staff meeting, we debriefed the evening.

"What did you see or observe?" was one of my questions to the staff. The first response was, "As we sat in that natural position on the stool (leaning slightly forward), I saw some of them (congregation) move to the front edge of their seat and lean forward toward us." Another staff member chimed in laughing, "I saw that too." At least half of the staff had recognized this seeming phenomenon. Even your posture can encourage and enthuse others.

Every coach should learn to read and communicate good posture when seated and standing. Your posture will communicate to the person(s) seated in front of you. How you sit, where you sit communicates to others. In my office if I want to have a person open up to me and receive endearingly what I have to offer, I do not sit behind my desk. I sit in front of my desk in a chair the same as the one they are seated in. I position the chairs facing in toward each other at about forty-five-degree angle. Chairs facing straight on can relay an uncomfortable air of interrogation.

If, on the other hand, I need to give a more forcible critique, or reprimand, I may sit behind the desk. Why? Because in this scenario I may want the other person to remember and realize who is in the seat of power. This is what a desk does, signifying authority. And your posture plays a big part in this scenario as well. Slouching posture does not convey power or leadership. To use a power-play like this is not a first step. Before, I move to this type meeting, you can know that this person has been in private meetings with me prior to this one. Meetings where I have sat in front of the desk alongside him as mentioned in the above paragraph. This and other power-play positions should be avoided and only used in necessary situations.

Communication of the Legs and Feet

The final part of body language that I want to write about for your coaching and leadership skills development is the lower extremities, the legs and feet. As a person is both seated and standing his/her legs and feet are communicating. The legs and feet are possibly the parts of our bodies that we are least aware of our communication factors. In other words, people are more apt to be aware of their own facial expressions, eye contact, and hand motions, than they are with what the feet and legs are conveying. For the coach and astute leader this means we should learn to pay attention to what the lower extremities are communicating.

A person may contort her face to appear to be listening and even interested. But if her feet are repeatedly tapping the floor or her legs and knees are bouncing, rest assured, she is anxiously awaiting the opportunity to leave. Feet tapping, knees bouncing are communicators that we do not want to be in the situation or meeting at hand. It is an outward expression of a subconscious desire to flee, as a cartoon character's legs spinning rapidly in place before taking off chasing another character. I've noticed the toe tapping and knee bouncing often to be more obvious in men. Yet, it is an involuntary reaction of women as well.

When seated many people have a tendency to cross their legs. There are three basic leg crossing styles. 1) The knee over knee – one leg on floor, the other crossed over with lower leg pointing down as well. 2) The 4 cross (also known as the figure 4)– one leg crossed over the other with shoe sole facing out instead of down. Looking from above, down on this crossing of the legs resembles a numerical four (4). This is more commonly used by men in the western hemisphere. 3) Crossed at the ankles. Each one of these acts as a communicator of behavior and emotional processing in the moment.

The knee over knee is the most used crossing of legs by women. Most often this is a gesture of modesty and concealment. Depending on other body language indicators, it can also demonstrate other communication factors as well. Men sitting knee over knee position are considered relaxed with an air of self-confidence. He is comfortable with himself and the conversation at hand. Certainly, this can be true of women seated in this position as well.

The 4 cross leg position is interesting as it is most common in the western hemisphere and seen only infrequently in European nations or older cultures. Sitting in the 4 cross position is a subconscious sign of dominance and can signal argumentative or aggressive attitudes. Men will shift to this position when feeling competitive, aggressive, or driven. The competitive spirit in men manifests itself through this type of dominant body language indicators. Since it is a subconscious action, most men will never realize what they may be communicating.

Today, the 4 cross is being recognized in other cultures where American culture has some influence. However, it is said that during World War II the Nazi's actually watched for men sitting in the 4 cross position. Any person sitting in this position was not a German or had spent considerable time in America. Apparently, someone in the Nazi regime recognized the significance of subconscious behavior revealed through body language.

Men and women sitting with legs crossed at the ankles are sending different signals. When men sit with legs crossed at the ankles, their feet are usually pulled back under the chair. Men sitting with ankles crossed have their legs spread open from hip to knee and begin to narrow from knee to ankle. This is similar in communication to the 4 cross. Using more leg space is a dominance communicator.

Women sitting with ankles crossed are subconsciously narrowing their occupation of leg space. Women sitting with legs crossed at the ankles pull their legs together, not apart as their counterpart, men.

In job interviews most every interviewee will at some point cross their legs at the ankles. When the interviewee also pulls his/her legs back, under the chair, this is associated with holding something back. Sometimes it may be withholding information. Many times it is holding back an emotion or behavior similar to biting nails or bouncing legs. When a person shifts in a conversation (interview or coaching session) to a legs pulled back and crossed at the ankles, it is likely they are withholding something. Using the right types of questions can assist the coachee in releasing the ankle cross and the needed information. You will learn more about this in the next section of this book. Use caution and do not draw attention to their sitting position or body language. When someone becomes aware of their body language, he/she cannot focus on the subject at hand.

Whether standing or sitting, our feet and legs communicate much about what the mind is thinking. A person's feet will point to where the brain is wanting to go. Men standing with legs apart, feet squared in front of them are again demonstrating a dominance trait. You will often find a group of men talking socially or in a casual business conversation all positioned in this dominant stance. It is as if they are each displaying their role as the "alpha" male. If one man is standing with one foot pointed in a slightly different direction, look to see what is in that direction, the exit, the food table, bar, or perhaps a woman. The feet point to where our mind wants us to go.

Reading Clusters

I have mentioned reading clusters several times thus far in the preceding pages of this book. In my experience, I have found that relying on one body language indicator will often lead to a misreading of the emotion or attitude behind the communication. Therefore, I now attempt to read body language through a cluster of indicators. A cluster is simply two or more parts of the body revealing a particular emotional or behavioral response. A person may be speaking of her boss using unbiased verbiage. But if her hands are closed (as if making a fist) and her eyebrows drawn inward and down, she likely does not consider her boss a friend or friendly.

Learning to read clusters may take some time. When learning to read clusters, my suggestion is to begin by observing the obvious or larger body communicators first. What are the arms and hands communicating? Remember, the arms and hands are usually the largest, loudest non-verbal communicators of the body. Next, the face. The face is always communicating when someone is speaking or silent. Since eye contact is of great importance, you'll be observing facial expressions with greater focus and larger blocks of time than other body communicators. The arms and hands will reveal information to you at a glance. The face on the other hand, can change quickly and frequently, so it requires more attention. It is wise to remember that many facial expressions are involuntary. We cannot control some of these, though they are very quick and fleeting.

Is the facial expression communicating a likeness to what the shoulders and hands are communicating? If you're unsure, take a quick look at the legs and feet. How are they positioned? Is he sitting in a defensive position such as the 4 cross? When a man is sitting with his legs in a 4 cross and his arms folded across his chest, take notice of his chin. Is it lowered. If so, this cluster is revealing this man has closed himself off. His arms legs and chin are in a defensive position as if defending parts of the body.

When a person's legs are crossed at the ankle and pulled back under his chair with his arms folded over the chest, this person is uninterested and likely bored with what is being communicated. Also, when the legs are stretched out in front of the person and crossed at the ankles, you will notice his sitting posture has also slouched. His arms will likely be folded across chest as well. This person is definitely uninterested and bored. If a person's feet are pointed in the same direction as the shoulders are turned, where is this person already headed in her mind?

Clusters can confirm what is being communicated. They may or may not back up the words being spoken. Clusters will give you indicators of true emotional beliefs about the subject being discussed. In learning to read body language clusters, work on one body part at a time. Perhaps beginning with learning some of the basic facial expressions while listening to voice inflection and tone. Because you are aware of upper body communication, you will begin to recognize some of the more visible communicators coming from the upper body. While practicing your own eye contact, learn to use your breaking eye contact glances to quickly view shoulders, arms and hands.

You will find, in time, that you will very seldom need to look at a person's legs, as leg indicators are larger and more visible. With time, in many scenarios, your eyes will take in leg communicators without looking down. Even then, you may want to look to his/her feet every few minutes to see where they are pointing. Learning to read body language clusters will greatly assist you in becoming a worthy, effective coach.

Body Language Wrap-up

There is much more we could explore about the legs, feet, and all of the parts of body language communicators. But for the sake of time and space, I have attempted to focus on a few communicators that will assist you as a coach and leader in moving your coachees and employees toward improving their performance and moving them to their greatest productivity, fulfilling their God-given purpose.

What I have written in this body language section can assist you in being a worthy, effective coach. I trust what you have read in the early pages of this book will encourage you to research other materials on identifying and reading these body language communicators. After all your brain may do your thinking, but your entire body is constantly communicating. Be the best communicator and reader of communication you can. Be a lifelong learner.

Chapter Seven

The Importance of Formulating the Right Question

"The scientist is not a person who gives the right answers, he's one who asks the right questions." Claude Lévi-Strauss

There is not much that I find more intriguing in the professional realm than studying and reading body language and deeper listening skills. The one thing that I am most passionate about is questions. To be more exact, my passion is the proper use of questions. Questions have been used since the beginning of time. However, in today's cultures more often than not, the wrong questions are being asked. It is true. In interviews, coaching sessions, Bible study groups, planning meetings, we are asking the wrong questions. Many times we are asking the wrong type of questions.

Perhaps the greatest tool God has given us for leadership and teaching is the question. Throughout history, the question has been unequivocally used in learning and leadership. Two thousand years ago, Jesus was using questions to lead, teach, and equip His followers and all who attended His "seminars." In chapter four of *Teaching That Bears Fruit*[iii] I reference several of His interactions using questions. With His use of questions, Jesus proved to be a Master Teacher and Leader. We can learn to use questions in the same manner.

For more than thirty years I have been a student of the question. Through the years my studies have included the various types of questions, the wording of questions, delivery techniques of questions, voice tone and inflection, even the emotion of a question. I never want to lose my drive, my thirst for learning more about the proper use of questions. My reason is two-fold. First, I want to be a lifelong learner. Second, the more I can learn, the more I grow in my ability to help others.

As a coach and leader, learning to use the right type of question formulated properly will be the determining factor of success in moving your client forward. Being able to properly formulate the right type of question and deployment of each question with perfect timing and order is more critical in moving a coachee forward than his response to your question. Let that sink in for a moment. Your coachee's success is more determined on your choice and delivery of questions than on his own response.

If you are not asking the right questions, your clients are not going to be able to give the response needed to take them on the desired path for fulfilling their purpose. Example: One question used too often and too quickly is, "What would it take to get there?" This is used when a client gives any of the following information. I can't seem to... get my desk cleaned off...get my to do list completed...keep my house clean. It may sound like, "What would it take to get there?" is a proper question to ask, right? To many people, it really does sound pertinent. In my opinion, it is not that this is a wrong question so much as it is wrong timing for the question.

A better question is to first use the "tell me more" approach. When someone tells me he can't seem to accomplish everything on his to do list, I want more information. I train coaches to not use the words, "tell me more". Instead, I use and train people to use phrases as, "Unpack that for me." Or Explain what you mean in more detail." Or "How would you explain that to someone who does not know your work environment?" I want him to "unpack" his thoughts before I ask him "what would it take..." Asking the "What would it take..." question too early and you might not get the necessary information to truly help your coachee. Asking too quickly, before you have all the needed information, and his response is likely to be, "I need more time, or I need my boss to hire some help."

I sent a young, new youth minister to spend a few days with a friend who has developed a strong youth ministry and has helped others in building and solidifying their ministry. In my debriefing conversation with the experienced coach, he told me that one of the first things the young man had said was he did not have time to do everything required of his position. He also said he knew he was not spending enough time studying and it was hurting his ministry.

His coach, Barry, did not ask the "What would it take" question at that time. It was too early. Instead Barry, asked questions that led the coachee to reveal how he spent his time. One thing revealed was this young man stayed up late into the night (early morning hours) playing video games. Therefore, he was too tired to study in the morning and came into the office wore out, before starting his day. By the time he returned home at night, you guessed it, he was too tired to study. But not too tired to play video games until two or three o'clock in the morning.

It wasn't until this information was revealed by the coachee that Barry asked a question to lead to a desired resolve of the issue in this young man's life. That first question was followed by a line of questions to assist the coachee in building a better day making the most of his time. Most of us will not have two to three consecutive days to work with a client as Barry did with this young man. Still, asking the "What would it take..." question too quickly, will start you down a path with the coachee, that may lead in a wrong direction. Asking the right questions is more than timing and evoking an answer. Asking the right questions with correct timing will lead you to be a worthy, effective coach, leading your clients to a more productive fulfillment of purpose.

Higher Level Thinking

I believe an imperative for a teacher or coach is understanding the importance of engaging the higher order thought processes of those sitting in front of you. As a coach, leader, or teacher, I must engage your higher order thought processes if I expect you to gain anything from our conversation, meeting, or study session. Just what are these higher order thought processes?

Much of the thinking we use every day relies on static recall, not deeper level thinking. Static recall is reaching into the memory bank. But it does not stimulate portions of the brain which cause us to learn or process new information. Static Recall Example: What day of the week is today? To answer this, you needed to engage your brain to recall something you already have in your memory bank. However, it did not engage your brain in a learning exercise.

Cognitive learning example: What does Saturday mean to you? To answer this question, you must engage more than static recall. It does indeed engage static recall as you must first determine what a Saturday is. But to answer the question, your brain must go into a deeper processing mode. Your brain begins to extract files of activities you do on Saturday. While doing this it also begins categorizing those activities into things you enjoy and those you do out of necessity, like yard work, laundry, house cleaning, etc. Our tendency is to file those things aside and begin focusing on the things we enjoy doing on Saturday, spending time with family, fishing, watching football.

All of this is happening in your brain at lightning speed. Your brain is processing thousands of pieces of material you've collected over the years. All of this is taking place in a few seconds to help you formulate a response. Since the brain processes information in this manner to help formulate a response, should we not take care to formulate the right questions?

Because the question was, "What does Saturday mean to you?" you will formulate a response by combining several of the pieces of information processed by your brain in those quick, few seconds. For many, it will be something they have never thought of or processed before. This one question has produced a learning experience for your coaching client. As a coach, I would then ask a question based off part of the client's response. It would be a question leading to his desired outcome; perhaps a more productive life, more time with family, etc. Example: "How do you guard your Saturday's so that you have that special time with your family?" or "What can you do to guard against scheduling things that take you away from your family on Saturday?"

Engaging the higher order thought processes is the only way we can attach new information to what already exists in our memory bank. Learning does not occur when using static recall. If we cannot attach the new information to something we already know, learning cannot take place. When we use questions that engage the higher order thought processes in a group setting, the brain of every person in the room engages. As one person responds verbally, all the others continue to process information including what is being spoken. Even if only three out of 36 people speak, each person in the room is experiencing a learning encounter.

As a coach, leader, or teacher you must learn to actively engage the higher order thought processes of your listeners. Now that the wheels are turning in your own brain, it is time to think on formulating good thought provoking questions that will engage the higher order thought processes and provide behavioral life-changing opportunities for your clients/students.

Formulating Good Thought Provoking Questions

Properly formulating questions is crucial in creating an atmosphere of discovery and a learning experience. Before we get into questions, let me first address why we need a discovery process in our coaching. Discovery learning is one of our God-given natural learning abilities[iv]. People learn best when they discover answers for themselves. As a coach, you need the coachees to think through the matters at hand so they can discover the real issues. Once discovery occurs people are more likely to have a desire and motivation to work toward needed change.

If you go into a church, organization, or any coaching situation giving all the facts, information, and a list of suggestions needed for change, you are not coaching. You have become a manager. Your role is not to manage. People being managed will not think for themselves. Neither will they act for themselves. Participation will quickly dissolve even before implementation begins. People need to discover answers for themselves. We, as coaches need to develop questions and arrange information in ways to engage the higher order thought processes of all our coachees whether we are coaching one on one or an entire organization.

Formulating good thought-provoking questions may take some practice, but it will be well worth the investment of your time and effort. Regardless of the information, facts, or statements you are reviewing, ask yourself, "How can this information (facts or statement) be used to create higher order thinking in our next meeting?" That, in fact, is a good example of the type questions you want to develop. It is certainly an open-ended question.

There is no simple, one way only, answer. You can come at it from different angles and perspectives. The question causes you to think and to look into the material being addressed from different approaches.

A good open ended question will promote higher order thinking (deep thinking) from everyone in the room; causing people to look at the information or issue from different viewpoints and approaches. Never ask a question you do not want someone else to answer. In other words, never answer your own question. Also, do not ask a question and move on without giving an opportunity to field responses from others in the room. Sometimes, you may need to re-ask your question or change the wording to give better clarification.

Using How, What, and Where questions are possibly easiest to formulate for good thought promoting discussion. Using Why to begin a question perhaps requires the most caution. "Why" questions often lead to responses allowing people to live in the past and to pass blame. This type of question is generally not productive and can produce a negative atmosphere.

Why questions will put people on the defensive. When people are on the defensive they are guarded about what they say. Example: Why do you think your church is in the situation it is today? All those who have been in the church for a number of years, will take a defensive approach. Most will start playing the blame game. As a coach, you want to avoid the blame game. Certainly, How, What, and Where questions could also be posed leading to negative responses. But, in our American culture, beginning a question with the word "Why" leads to a defensive position – in words and body language. Try a why question on someone and watch his/her body language. They will tense up and assume a defensive posture even before you complete your question.

Instead of dealing in the past and the negative, find the positive or objective of the issue by looking to the future. Example: instead of, "Why do you think your church is in the situation it is today?" you want to ask, "In your opinion, what will a brighter future beyond this situation look like for your church?" This question causes everyone to think. Not about the past or negative issues, but about a brighter, positive future. As different people respond everyone in attendance is processing the information shared.

Perhaps as a coach you need your coachee(s) to examine the past. If so, what questions could you ask to get the discussion started without it turning into a gripe fest? Example: "What do you see as the biggest obstacle you need to overcome? If you are coaching in a group setting, you will want to set the ground rules. One of which is, your discussion cannot attack individuals, only issues.

Here are a few other sample starter questions.

How are we equipped as an organization to...? (example: discover the needs of the community)

What strengths do we have that can be used to...? (example: show the community God's love)

Where can we look to find...? (example: a partnership with the community)

What are you willing to do to see this through?

When would be a good time to launch...?

How would you suggest...?

What is the one thing you could...? (implement, say, create)

If we were to list...what is the one thing you would add to the list?

Why would moving in this direction be a good move for you (your organization)?

How could you involve more ministry groups of the church in....?

In what ways would you suggest we promote...?

In formulating good thought promoting questions, always think ahead. If I ask this question, what follow-up question(s) could I ask to keep the discussion going in the direction needed to make forward progress? You'll learn more about how to do this in chapter ten, The Funnel approach.

People do not like to be told anything, but they love to give their opinion and answer questions with their thoughts and experience. Therefore, use words and phrases such as, "In your opinion," and "What would you suggest..." This takes people off the defensive and immediately engages everyone's higher order thought processes.

Study and practice formulating and using open-ended questions. Become proficient at asking good open-ended thought promoting questions. Then continue to study. Become a student of the question. Learn to think in questions. It is a fun discovery learning way to live!

Chapter Eight

The Purpose of a Question

*"Life is filled with unanswered questions, but it is the courage to
seek those answers that continues to give meaning to life."*
J.D.Stroube

Have you ever considered the purpose of a question? If asked
on the street, most people would say the purpose of a question is
to get an answer. But, is this a benefitable purpose? Maybe if
you are asking for directions, it is. Even in this scenario, you are
receiving more than an answer. You are receiving valuable
information directing your path. Think on this: when you ask for
directions, you receive more than an answer – more than words.
You receive a mental picture of what lies ahead. You receive
intelligence that will lead you to a desired objective. This, in part,
is the art of the question.

Let me ask this question: Is it not shallow and superficial of us to
assume the only reason to ask a question is to get an answer?
God gave us the beauty of the question for much more than
simply to get an answer, as illustrated in the example above. The
purpose of a question cannot be explained in one short
definition. The purpose of the question is to unlock the
mysteries of the mind, heart, soul, and will of every person in
this world. The question is a beautiful God-given masterpiece. It
is a palette of amazing colors for painting works of genius in the
lives of those whom we interact.

In *Teaching That Bears Fruit*,[v] my first book, chapter four is titled *The Art of The Question*. When you ardently study the question, you learn that the question truly is a beautiful art form. Using properly formulated questions with correct timing you have the power to change someone's life. As a coach, you have a lifetime ahead of you geared toward changing lives. All through the power of questions. With each question, you are providing the paint with which your coachees will be applying each stroke of the brush onto the masterpiece of his and her life. This is the fulfillment of properly deploying great questions.

But what is the purpose of the question? Questions are used to fulfill several purposes. Properly formulated questions asked at the right time, in the right manner can 1) gather information, 2) substantiate a person's prior knowledge of a subject, 3) solicit your listener's approval, 4) promote higher level thinking which leads to true behavioral learning and life change. As a coach and a leader all four of these will assist you in leading your coachee/employee to life purpose fulfillment.

Gather Information

This is perhaps the most widely used motive for asking questions, to gather information. We ask what time it is. Why? Because we want to know that information. Perhaps we are on a schedule and do not want to be late. We ask what the weather is like outside. Why? Because that information will help us prepare before stepping outdoors. We ask how long a person has been in a particular position. Why? Because we believe that information may be pertinent to our conversation. We ask for directions (at least women do) because that information is going to lead us to our desired destination.

We've been using questions to gather information since the beginning of spoken languages. Think of the conversations you've had in your day, today or yesterday. Even the shortest and most brief of encounters likely involved the use of questions to invoke information. How are you doing today? (okay, maybe that one is mostly used as a courtesy) But it does request information. Many of our interactions with other people involve the use of questions. Most of these questions are to gather information.

As a coach this type question is fundamental in our approach to assist the coachee or organization. A worthy coach almost always begins with an information gathering question. "What do you want to talk about today?" or "What has happened since our last meeting?" This is not only an information gathering question. It is the foundation upon which you will build the entire coaching session. Not only is it fundamental for building the session, but also in building the foundation for part of the coachee's life for the next increment of weeks (four weeks, six weeks) until your next coaching session.

The first question in an interview or coaching session is not the only information gathering question we will use in the session. But it is foundational for building the remainder of the session. When your coachee has finished his response to your first "information gathering" question, the next words out of the coach's mouth are important to the success of the entire session. Oftentimes it is natural response to comment on what the coachee has said or to give an anecdote or illustration from your own life. This is a wrong response.

As a coach, you will serve your client better by using a "tell me more" inquiry. When a person stops. He/she feels he has given you all the information necessary. I want to encourage him to dig deeper. The "tell me more" or "unpack this for me" query is used in part for gathering information. It is digging deeper. However, the 'tell me more" portion of your session is for more than gathering information. It is in response to this question that a coachee may begin to unearth the needed resolve – what it is going to take to resolve the real issue. It is in many such scenarios that you will be able to direct your coachee's thinking. It is here that we often find he has the information necessary to tackle the situation at hand. That information just may need to be unearthed and packaged differently.

It is vital for a worthy coach to comprehend the information being given – along with the body's communication – in this first interaction of each session. Asking the coachee to "unpack" the information gives you greater information gathering opportunities. It will also lead you to a right path for the remainder of the session. Information gathering questions set the base and foundation for assisting the coachee.

Substantiate Prior Knowledge

Questions are also used to determine the level of knowledge a person has coming into a particular situation or study topic. This is often used in class settings, when a teacher wants to understand what class participants know about the subject to be discussed in class. Job interviewers use this to gain an understanding of the interviewee's knowledge of the company and the job being interviewed for. There is not a strong need to pursue a long interviewing process for an accounting position with a woman who does not know basic bookkeeping or how to balance her checkbook.

As a coach you can use questions as, "What do you know about...?" However, a different approach, to engage the higher order thought processes could be, "If you were to...?" Example: You are coaching a leader and know he is about to make a decision. Understanding that you also need to assist him in "rolling out" his decision to his direct reports and everyone in his corporation or congregation, your line of questioning could be: "If you were to draw concentric circles of how you will spread this to your entire organization, who would you place in each circle?"

You might draw or better yet have your coachee draw a series of circles with an x in the middle of the smallest circle and each circle a little larger encircling the smaller ones. You could state,

"You are the X. In your organization, who makes up this first circle of need to know?" Once this person or group is named, move to the next circle. Repeat this until everyone in the organization has potentially been made aware of the decision.

What you have done with this coaching exercise is engaged his higher order thought processes. The leader must process the best way to get the information out to everyone. This requires more than static recall. Since you are present you can ask questions if you see a breach in information sharing due to misaligned organization or missing connections to people groups within the organization. This leader already has the information inside his head. You are asking the question and using this exercise to unearth the proper channels for dissemination. You are using a question to substantiate prior knowledge by inquiring on his knowledge of the organization "chain of command" and his understanding of communicating down to the lowest level of information dissemination.

It is difficult to assist a person (or organization) until you understand her knowledge level of both the situation at hand and the resources necessary to move forward. Time will be better served if you do not allow your coachee to linger on past failures or trouble spots. Opening these up for clarity and for the purpose of moving forward can be beneficial. Lingering there and wallowing in them is not beneficial and serves only as a time waster and negative fuel source. As a coach, it is very beneficial to substantiate prior knowledge, allowing you to assist in building on this knowledge base.

Soliciting Your Listener's Approval

Questions are also used to solicit the approval of others, wouldn't you agree? If not, then the first question in this paragraph is invalid, isn't it? So would be the second one rendered invalid. In other words, the first two sentences of this paragraph are not sentences, but questions. Both of these questions are soliciting your approval. Whether in a formal classroom setting or a casual conversation, we all use questions to solicit our listener's approval. For some, we want to know that our listeners agree with us. Other times we need to know that our listeners understand the information being shared before moving on. It will do no good to explain how a combustion engine works if our listener has no idea what a combustion engine is.

Another means for using this is to ask questions which solicit your coachee's approval on what they have shared with you. Example: Let's say you are coaching a young lady who has shared how she feels overworked and underappreciated. She in fact, has spent the previous five minutes sharing her feelings and examples on the subject. As a coach you might begin your questioning with, "If I am hearing you correctly, you believe that you and three others carry the weight of your organization, correct?" While this appears to be a yes or no question, it has been worded in a manner that will ninety (90) percent of the time engage the higher order thought processes.

Your coachee's first response might be yes. And I have found in many such scenarios, this yes is followed by an explanation. The explanation is most often a "tell me more" response. By soliciting your coachee's approval, you have also triggered her higher thinking skills into digging deeper. I have heard responses as, "Yes. But let me explain. Not in everything, I guess. But we do carry the weight in..." By soliciting her approval, you have helped her "unpack" more of the reality of the situation. In turn, this gives you, the coach, more information for discerning the necessary path of the session.

In chapter nine, you will read about the statement question. I guess I would have to say I have a special fascination with the statement question and properly using it in teaching and leadership. Using a question to solicit your listener's approval almost always employs the use of a statement question. Learning to use these to solicit the amount of learning and approval is beneficial to any leader and coach. Teaching others to use these is downright fun.

Promote Higher Level Thinking

Perhaps the most valid and transforming purpose of all questions is to engage the listener in a behavioral life-changing experience. Before this type of learning experience can take place, a person must have his/her higher order thought processes engaged. Review chapter seven for engaging higher order thought processes of your coachees, clients, volunteers, and students.

In most settings, in the corporate world, in the church, and other learning environments we have relegated our questions to only engage static recall. Static recall produces no true learning. It is only regurgitating what we already know. Asking yes or no questions cannot produce learning. Instead of asking your coachee, "Did you start the new process we discussed last month?" Why not ask, "Can you tell me two steps you have taken in the past month to move toward the new process we discussed?"

The first question, "Did you start the new process we discussed last month?" only asks for a yes or no answer. Your coachee knows what he did or did not start. This question requires no thought process at all. Yes, I did, or No, I did not. The second question automatically engages the higher order thought processes whether he did or did not take steps.

Even if the coachee has not taken any steps, your question has automatically engaged his higher order thought processes. He will be thinking of what he has done, why he has not taken steps, and steps he knows he can take in the next thirty days. Which, the premise of the last part of that sentence should be one of your next questions. You may want to help him explore what obstacles kept him from moving forward. You certainly want to lead him to set goals for steps to take the next thirty days while avoiding those obstacles.

If he has begun implementing steps for a new process, he will immediately begin processing what steps he has taken. His mind is already engaged in positive steps. He is open and ready for you to help him examine these steps and prepare for next steps.

Engaging one's higher order thinking is so very important and crucial to produce life-change learning. I truly desire you to understand this fact and become a student of engaging the higher order thought processes of those you coach, teach , and lead in every aspect of your life.

These are four purposes of questions. As a coach though, your main purpose is to ask questions that will lead to a behavioral life change. This type of life-change is the manifestation of true behavioral learning. True behavioral learning will move a person or group toward reaching their full potential as an individual or group. As you study and learn to properly use these four purposes of the question, may your own life be changed as you assist others. After all, helping others to have the courage to seek the answers to the right questions continues to give purposeful meaning to life.

Chapter Nine

Natures of the Question

"Furthermore, if questions so profoundly predetermine thought and inquiry, then it would seem to make sense to get them right lest our searching become a blind man's groping."
Unknown

As a worthy coach it is important to know and understand the varying natures of questions. In chapter seven we learned of the importance of using properly formulated questions with right timing. Then in chapter eight, you read about the purpose of the question. The next thing to know regarding using the right question at the right time is understanding the natures of questions. And yes, natures is plural. Different questions have different natures. Nature is defined as the inherent character of a person or thing[vi]. As a coach and leader, we need to understand the inherent (in-built) character of a question.

The inherent character of a question will largely determine the response. I believe there are four basic natures of questions. These are: 1) Closed ended, 2) Open ended, 3) Rhetorical, and 4) Statement. Each nature solicits a different mode of response. One of these natures cause the listener to use static recall, not engaging the higher order thought processes. The other three cause the listener's brain to activate the cognitive skills of the brain, engaging the higher order thought processes described in chapter seven.

Closed Ended Questions

We will begin with the type of question that produces the least amount of learning. Though it produces little or no learning, this is the one question type most used in society and in our learning institutes (schools, churches, organizations, management meetings) today. The name of this question type demonstrates its nature. This question type which produces the least amount of learning, and often no learning at all is the closed ended question. A closed ended question only engages the static recall section of the brain. Remember, static recall pulls information, facts, and figures already stored in the brain, and produces no brain activity that will produce learning.

The response for a closed ended question is most often a one word or one sentence factual or historical statement. Questions that call for a yes or no answer are indeed closed ended questions. "Have you shared your experience with someone?" is a closed ended question. This question could lead to better questions, but why not start with the better questions. Also, this question could put the responder on the defensive. When a person's thought process turn to the defensive, seldom will he/she be able to appropriately process information vital to moving forward. This causes the coaching process to stall out during the discussion.

In a coaching or any leadership experience, you should guard against the use of closed ended questions. Certainly, there are times when closed ended questions are relevant. But, in my experience they should be rare, and when used, closed ended questions should be geared to allow you to follow up with questions to move the coachee, employee, or volunteer forward toward his greatest potential avoiding defensiveness.

When is a closed ended question appropriate? Only when you are seeking a particular piece of information, a specific fact or figure. Even in this scenario, the piece of information you are fishing for, should lead to an open door for leading the coachee forward. Example: You are speaking with a person whose department is falling short of production so you ask, "What were your production numbers last month?" This is a closed ended question. It requests a specific piece of information. Delivering the information produces no learning for the coachee. But it does open a door for you to begin asking relevant questions to engage the higher order thought processes of the coachee, which could lead to higher productivity.

Closed ended questions rely on static recall only and generally are answered with one word (yes, no, 10, midnight) or one sentence answers. Once a closed ended question is answered, everyone's thinking shuts down. There is no longer a need to think. It matters not how many people are in the room. The person whose relfex and recall are the quickest answers and there is no need for anyone to think any longer. Everyone in the room has removed his/her thinking cap.

It takes time, but you can train yourself to avoid closed ended questions in many scenarios. Today, if a closed ended question comes to mind, I'll ask myself how can this be reworded to assist the coachee or student in becoming more effective. Learning to restrict the use of closed ended questions will render you a greater effectiveness as a worthy coach and bring your coachees closer to fulfilling their God-given potential.

Open Ended Questions

The opposite of a closed ended question, naturally would be an open-ended question. Open ended questions allow the brain to engage in higher processing modes rather than static recall only. The names of these two question types reveal their nature. A closed ended question does not engage the higher order thought processes, keeping that portion of the brain closed. An open-ended question on the other hand, opens and engages the cognitive memory, recall, and creative portions of the brain. Media College.com on their website says the following about open ended questions. "An open-ended question is designed to encourage a full, meaningful answer using the subject's own knowledge and/or feelings."[vii]

"Designed to encourage"- isn't this what art is about? When you encourage, you leave an impression. Painters paint with the hope of encouraging others. Performers sing to encourage others with words and melody. Properly formulating and deploying the right questions is truly an art form. And there is no question better at making a lasting impression than the open-ended one.

Whether you are speaking one on one or in a room of thousands, deploying an open-ended question causes the mind of every person listening to open the cognitive portion of the brain. When an open-ended question is posed, the auditory sensors send the incoming message to the brain. The cognitive sensory patterns open and the brain begins processing the incoming information first pulling the pieces of known information (facts, figures, images). Example: When I ask, "What is your favorite pen to write with?" Your brain recognized the words favorite and pen. Your memory bank, within a mili-second, began pulling together photos of ink pens you've known and used. Most people reading that question even saw at least one ink pen in your own hand.

As this is happening, all these images are rushing through, the word "favorite" began to filter each one. Perhaps you didn't land on a "favorite" pen from your past. What your mind did instead is create a pen that made you feel comfortable in your hand. One that would be your favorite. Your brain even chose the color for you. How did your brain know which color to choose? Your "favorite." It chose a favorite of yours. Perhaps your favorite color, or a color you are very accustomed to being around (school or sports team's color). The brain is an amazing apparatus and amazingly quick! And now, you have a favorite pen.

If I were standing in a room speaking to one thousand people and asked this question, each person in the room would be processing the same way. Each one would come up with the correct answer. And yet, each answer would be different in some regard. To formulate a response or answer to an open-ended question, a person must have something in his/her knowledge base to build on (pen, favorite). Once this information is pulled from the memory bank, the brain begins to construct the new sought after information. Many people have never thought about having a favorite pen. Now, once that newly formed information has been calculated, it will be stored in the memory bank. A learning experience has taken place.

Open ended questions will cause every person in the room to engage his/her higher order thought processes. When the speaker, coach, teacher, then calls for responses each person continues their contemplation, weighing each response with his own. Bill, in the front of the room says "A green fountain pen." Everyone who has knowledge of a fountain pen, instantly ponders this and makes a decision if they agree or disagree – for their own pen, not Bill's. Perhaps, Jim in the back of the room thinks, "What is a fountain pen?" What kind of images just popped into Jim's mind? Whether one or twenty-one people respond, everyone in the room will continue using their higher order thought processes until the speaker moves them to another idea or topic.

Learning to use open ended questions is vital to any coach, leader, and teacher. Without the proper use of good open-ended questions, you will never move any person to his/her greatest level of learning and achievement. You will find sample open-ended questions in the appendix section of this book. Remember, an open-ended question cannot be answered with yes, no, or any other one word or simple sentence of information. Open-ended questions engage the higher order thought processes of everyone in the room.

Rhetorical Questions

The third nature of a question is the Rhetorical. A rhetorical question is one asked where a response is not expected. A *rhetorical question* is asked for emphasis or to make a point on some element being discussed. No real answer is expected. Though no answer is expected for a rhetorical question, they are used to stimulate thought, beyond static recall. Some rhetorical questions have the answer in the question itself. Other times a rhetorical question is used as a challenge to the listener. A third way a rhetorical question is used is to raise doubt.

Certainly, you've been asked a rhetorical question with the answer inside the question, right? If not before, that question is such a question. It is a question and the answer is in the question. Certainly you have. We've all been asked this type question. And we've asked them of others. This is likely the most used type of rhetorical question. Parents ask, "Didn't I tell you not to eat any cookies before dinner?" This is a rhetorical question with the answer in the midst. We also use this type of question in everyday speech. "Is the sky blue and grass green?" "Does a pig squeal?" "Nice weather, isn't it?" In a coaching session we might ask, "So your job is to flip the thingamajig into a whatchamacallit?" The information has already been shared. While an answer is not necessary, you are engaging the coachee's mind for recollection and clarification. You are stating the answer inside the question.

A rhetorical question can be used to issue a challenge to someone. Perhaps you've heard someone ask a friend, "Have you looked at yourself in the mirror lately?" This type of rhetorical question can easily be used in a coaching session. A worthy coach understands and employs questions that will challenge the coachee out of his/her comfort zone. I have listened as people make statements such as, "I don't have any talents at all." A rhetorical challenge question could be, "You don't really believe that?" This is a rhetorical question in that I don't necessarily expect an answer. But, I do want the other person to think about what he just said – the true reality. Because the true reality is everyone has talents. We just don't all have the same talents. If we did, you and 100 other people would've written this book before I got around to it.

When I ask, "You don't really believe that?" Because I phrased it as a question, the coachee's mind kicks into gear. His higher order thought processes are engaged. Once engaged, I can follow up with a question to assist the coachee in unearthing his talents. I can use those same five words as a statement and move on. "You don't really believe that." But then I would have missed a great, and much needed learning opportunity for the coachee. Your mind is trained to stop and engage when something is formed as a question. In print if it has a question mark at the end, or in verbal language when my voice intonation signals an inquiry, something in your brain triggers the cognitive responders. It's as if there is a trigger in your brain for questions. A sentence with a period at the end and your brain says keep going. The same sentence with a question mark and your brain says, "Stop, something to process." As a coach it is imperative that we issue challenge questions to our coachees.

The third way to use a rhetorical question is to raise doubt. The question we used in the example above could be used to raise doubt as well. In the above scenario, the person already had doubt. So we would use, "You don't believe that?" as a challenge. On the other hand, if someone is spreading gossip as if it were gospel, we might use those same four words to infuse doubt. Choose your voice inflection and intonation wisely. It is not always what you say as much as how you say it.

Rhetorical questions should be used with the intent of causing the coachee to engage his/her higher thought processes concerning a point or idea being discussed. Rhetorical questions can be used to bring about reflection, clarification, remembrance, challenge and doubt. Learning to use properly formulated rhetorical questions at the right time will enhance your ability as a worthy coach and jumpstart your clients toward reaching their potential.

Statement Question

The fourth nature of a question is similar to a rhetorical question, but can be used in a variety of ways. The best way to define a statement question is to say any statement can be turned into a question, can't it? I just did it, didn't I? That's two in a row, isn't it? That made three, doesn't it? And now four. I could go on and on, because truly any statement can be turned into a question. Children use these with their parents all the time, don't they? Okay, that's the last one – maybe. Children do use them. So do salesmen. This is where I first learned of the statement question, in sales. Sales people are trained to listen for statements that can be turned into a question, moving the customer toward making a purchase. If you never realized this happening to you, I promise every time you have considered a big ticket purchase, a salesman has used this tactic on you.

Coaches and Bible study teachers need to hone their skills on this nature of a question. While serving as minister of education in three different churches I would meet with our adult class teachers on Wednesday. Our purpose was to review and prepare the upcoming week's lesson. Each week I would print out a one page bullet outline of thoughts and questions for us to review about the lesson. In all three churches someone (a different person each week) would inherently make an inquiry similar to, "This is a good question. Where did you get it?" I would smile, at least on the inside and say something like, "Turn to page 63 in your leader's guide.

On page 63 we would find the same wording. Only instead of a question it would be written as a sentence. At times, they could not understand. How could they have read it earlier in the week and not pay attention to it? The explanation is, our brains are trained in grammar. When your brain sees a period at the end of a sentence, it says, go on, keep reading. However, when your brain sees a question mark, it is trained to say, stop, wait a second. There is something to ponder here. The same is true when I verbally ask a question. A question engages a different portion of the brain for response. This is why it is so important to learn to formulate proper questions. Because as a coach or leader, you want to move the coachee forward.

As mentioned earlier statement questions can be used in a variety of ways. Here are eight. Statement questions can be 1) rhetorical. But they can also be used to 2) gain information, as 3) tell me more questions, 4) closed-ended, 5) open-ended, 6) bringing focus and alignment to the coachee, 7) ascertaining prior knowledge, and 8) acquiring your coachee's approval. I encourage you to practice forming a statement question for each one of the eight. There are more statement questions in the appendix section of this book.

Statement questions can often be closed ended. We must take care to keep them open or at least to use them to engage higher order thought processes. Example: "You went to the game but didn't watch it?" While on the surface this may look like a closed-ended, yes or no question. When asked it automatically engages the cognitive sensory of the brain. The brain begins to process the aspects of the venture to the game and why it was not seen. This almost always will employ more than static recall.

Statement questions can be fun. But we must take caution not to introduce our agenda or experiences into a question that would limit a coachee's growth. When used properly, statement questions can be very rewarding, leading to discovery learning. All of our questions should be geared to moving our coachees forward. Forward in discovery learning. This is what will enable our coachee to reach for their greatest God-given potential. I encourage you to read this chapter a second and third time. Then review it once a year. Also, purchase your copy of *Teaching That Bears Fruit* and read chapter four, *The Art of the Question*[viii]. Practice writing questions in each nature. Especially the last three. When you find yourself writing a closed ended question, ask yourself how to reword it for a learning experience.

Questions are truly a great gift from God. Learning the different natures of questions will lead you to be a worthy coach creating many discovery learning experiences for your coachees, peers, and others in your life. After all if questions so profoundly predetermine thought and inquiry, doesn't it make sense to get them right lest our searching become a blind man's groping?

Chapter Ten

Deploying Questions Using The Funnel

" We get wise by asking questions, and even if these are not answered, we get wise, for a well-packed question carries its answer on its back as a snail carries its shell."
James Stephens

It is good to remember when coaching you are going to be asking a series of questions. You are not attempting to solve an issue or change a situation with just one magic bullet question. There are no magic bullet questions. As a worthy, effective coach, we listen, ask, listen again, ask, listen, ask. This is the role of a coach. With each question you listen to evaluate if the coachee is moving in the desired direction. And each question is designed and formulated to assist the coachee in making forward progress toward a desired goal. If you believe your coachee is not giving an answer toward forward progress, then it is your obligation to shift the gears of the conversation – with a question.

Shifting the conversation sometimes is as simple as re-asking the question. "I understand that is how you feel, but the question is, 'What about her actions caused you to distrust her?'" It is easy for people to get side-tracked with feelings. These will be revealed not only in their verbiage, but also through body language. Recirculating the question should be done in a fashion that causes the coachee to refocus on the issue at hand. In this case the cause of the distrust issue.

Another way to bring this refocus is to reword the question. "Good. That explains how you feel and that you distrust her. Can you describe what specifically she did that brought you to this point of distrust?" You are reaching for the same information, simply worded differently. This can be used to redirect the coachee's attention away from feelings he seems to be centered on.

Still a third way to redirect this coachee's focus is to approach with a different line of questioning. "In what other relationships, in the past, have you experienced this type of distrust?" Again, this question is used to redirect the coachee's attention away from his feelings toward this one particular person whose actions brought about the distrust issues. Your question is actually asking the individual to begin an internal investigation at his role in the distrust issue. His response may reveal a vulnerability or weakness. It could also reveal a control issue or sense of power and struggle with releasing power.

Each of the three questions used above is deployed with you, the coach's, expectation of following up with another question subsequent to your coachee's response. Every question asked should lead to a narrowing toward a point of decision making. In other words, you use his response from the first question to formulate a second question which will lead your coachee in the direction of forward progress – arriving at the proper conclusion.

Coach: "In what other relationships, in the past, have you experienced this type of distrust?"

Coachee: "I had not thought about it before, but there was a similar issue with..."

Coach: "So, are you beginning to see a pattern based on these three relationships you have discussed?"

Coachee: "Yes, I'm apparently not real good at picking women for this type of relationship."

Coach: "Let's look at it from a different angle. Could it be not the women but a vulnerability of your character?"

Coachee: "I don't understand?"

Coach: "Well, from what you've told me, I'm curious. Could it be that you are expecting too much too quickly out of these relationships, placing undue stress on both you and these women?"

Coachee: "I never thought about that either. But listening to myself describe those other relationships, there are certainly some similarities in my actions leading up to my distrust."

Coach: "Okay what were those actions on your part?"

Coachee: "I wanted more time with each of these women. I didn't like their other friends getting time that I wanted to spend with each one...My actions may have forced each of these women to do what they did. I caused the distrust. I can see that now. It was as much me as it was them."

Coach: "Moving forward, what are you willing to do to curb this vulnerability you've discovered in yourself?"

Each question the coach asked in this scenario led to a response that allowed the coach to prepare a follow up question that would bring the coachee closer to the recognition of needed change and adjustment. Before any adjustment could be made, the coachee had to realize a need for adjustment. Before the realization of needed adjustment, the coachee must come to terms with where the breakdown is. In this scenario, the coachee came to the conclusion that it was he who was responsible for the breakdown. Without taking appropriate responsibility, one will never begin the rebuilding process – in any situation.

Regardless of what the topic of discussion and what path the coachee is taking in his discussion, you, as a worthy coach, must be prepared with a series of questions that by answering, he will come to a proper conclusion. A proper conclusion will always lead to a desired path for greater effectiveness. One question will never bring about a desired end result in a coaching situation. While your final question may bring the desired response, it is your first four to five questions which leads to the discovery experience in the final response.

In the coaching example above, about relationships, the coach began with a broader question to refocus the thought processes of the coachee. While the coach used a series of questions, he could not formulate the questions until the prior response. Still, each question brought the coachee a little closer to the needed conclusion – the proper decision.

Since my responsibility as a coach is to lead each of the coachees in a discovery learning process, I prefer to use what I refer to as the funnel approach. A funnel is described as a utensil that is usually a hollow cone with a short tube extending from the smaller end of the cone and that is designed to catch and direct a downward flow.

Every funnel has its widest point at the top or mouth of the funnel. From that opening the funnel tapers inward, getting progressively smaller in size until it reaches a narrow tube. Funnels are made to bring any substance flowing into it to a particular concentrated point (the tube). The purpose of a funnel is to bring such substance into a focal point, where it can be corralled for proper storage and use. A funnel is used to avoid spillage and undue splatter.

The funnel approach should be your most used tool in your coaches' toolbox. Don't miss this one. The funnel approach should be as handy to you as the hammer hanging on a carpenter's belt. And the funnel approach should be used as frequently as a carpenter uses his hammer.

Using the funnel approach, my first question may be very broad and open. Then, each ensuing question will narrow the scope leading the coachee in the direction necessary to reach his/her objective. Thus, bringing the discussion from a broad perspective into the tube of proper usage. The coaching exchange cited earlier in this chapter (relationships with women) used the funnel approach. The following is another example.

Coachee: "I just can't seem to get my office clean. I have stacks of paper on every corner of my desk and on the file cabinets."

Coach: "How would it change your work environment to have your office cleaned and straightened?"

Coachee: "It would be great. I think I could get more accomplished and I would certainly be more productive."

Coach: "What, in your opinion, would it take to get your office to that point?"

Coachee: "It would take a lot of time and I would really need to find time to clean it up."

Coach: "Okay, if you were to break that down into smaller segments, what would those be?"

In the example above you will notice the funnel process. The first question by the coach is more of a broad and open question. *"How would it change your work environment if...?"* The second question moves to what and brings the conversation into a focal point for the coachee. The focal point in this illustration is moving toward a clean office and productive work environment. The third question then fine tunes the focus. Each question brings the focus into a narrower and more manageable vision for the future. Just like a funnel, you are bringing the coachee to a focused and doable project for better effectiveness. In this scenario, a more productive work environment is the doable, focused project.

As the coachee responds to each question, you can always relate it back to the objective from his response to the first question – a more productive work environment. Look at the coachee's response to the second question; "It would take a lot of time and I would really need to find time to clean it up." Does this response relate to creating a more productive work environment? Certainly! He does not have time now, but he is admitting he would be more productive if he would take the time to clean up. This is what allowed the coach to move to question three. "Okay, if you were to break that down into smaller segments, what would those be?"

Let's say the coachee adds one sentence to his response to the first question. "It would take a lot of time and I would really need to find time to clean it up. I just don't have that time." Simply by adding that one statement "I just don't have the time." would warrant me as his coach to ask a question referring him back to his original response. I would likely ask something as, *"But, you do see that by taking that time it would create a much more productive work environment for you?"* You will notice this is a closed ended statement question with a caveat. It is closed ended, yet it will in most people engage the higher order thought processes as he begins to anticipate my next question – How. Once he responds to my question, "But you do see...?" then I am ready to proceed with the third question from our illustration above, "if you were to break that down into smaller segments, what would those be?"

At the beginning of each coaching session it is important for the coach and coachee to understand the objective for this session. In the scenario above, a more productive work environment. In the relationship example shown earlier in this chapter, it is finding the source for distrust of the coachee in his relationships. Once you understand the objective, it becomes easier to begin formulating your questions. Learning to use the funnel approach, gives you the opportunity to guide the coachee to unearth needed adjustments and necessary changes for a more effective and purposeful lifestyle.

Now, it's your turn. Get a piece of paper and pen, or use your computer and a word processor and write a four to five question funnel for the following exercises.

1 Your coachee states that he does not have enough time to accomplish his workload.

2 You are coaching a business owner who is having difficulty getting his managers to engage employees in lower level decision making processes. (or a pastor who is having difficulty getting his deacons on board with his vision)

Learning to use the funnel approach is perhaps one of the greatest tools you can use as a coach. But it takes time. It takes practice. Properly using the funnel approach will lead your coachees to the right decisions for their individual circumstances at the specific time you are coaching. You may coach the same person one year later in a different scenario with similar circumstances, but the needed adjustments may vary. The proper deploying of the funnel will guide to an effective purpose filled decision. Using the funnel the coachee does the heavy lifting (discerning). You as coach only point them toward that which needs to be lifted.

Epilogue

Putting it all together

Coaching, in my opinion, is a great gift from God. Coaching is God's greatest level of leadership. Unparalleled by any other I've witnessed in my lifetime. I do not want the credit for coaching. God alone gets the credit. There is no room in coaching for, "I told you so." The point of coaching is to destroy that statement by saying, "I didn't tell you. You discovered all this on your own – by the grace of God. All I did was listen and ask the right questions." As a coach it is never about me. It is about helping others find their God-directed path.

Several times over the past two years I have been asked by people around the nation to write this book (a book on coaching). Most of these requests came from men and women who have attended coach training that I've led and some who have grown into the coaching experience through our relationship of coach and coachee. For whatever reason, I held off for some time. After yet another request last fall, I finally broke down and prayed, "God I keep getting asked, is this what you desire. If so, it is your book Lord, not mine." Within a couple of hours I sat down at my computer and typed, *Coaching: A Way of Leadership, A Way of Life.*

Let me take a few paragraphs to share with you a small number of cautions and how to avoid making these common mistakes.

A coach is not a therapist. Keep the coaching relationship moving forward. Your interest is not about digging in the past. It is about keeping the conversation, and action plans moving the coachee forward to a more productive and effective purpose filled life. Every question you ask, every illustration you share, should be used to inspire the coachee to run toward a brighter future fulfilling his God-given purpose.

Resist the temptation to share your own experiences. Your experiences were right for you and your particular situation. Your coachee needs to find his own God directed path. Each of us has been created unique. Therefore, even when events and circumstances appear similar in our lives, each person's response and needs are different and unique. As a coach, your obligation is not to offer your decisions, but to lead the coachee to the best course of action for his/her life.

Refrain from the attraction to offer suggestions. Each person, organization, or team must come to their own decisions and build a working plan on their talents, skills, abilities, and experiences. Your suggestions are yours, not mine, not theirs. Each coachee must discover his own suggestions before ownership can be accepted. As a coach, your aim is to lead your coachees to discover the path which fits their giftings. Then you are to help them formulate a plan – their plan to move forward toward the desired goal. You accomplish this not by offering suggestions, but by asking the right questions, questions of discovery, and construction.

Pause before speaking. To be a good listener you must put away the natural tendency to prepare your rebuttal or response while the other person is speaking. Wait until he or she is finished speaking. Take a few seconds, gather your thoughts, then proceed with your next question. Too often we plan our response or next question within the first sixty seconds of listening. In doing this we easily miss the better opportunity to assist our coachee. What is verbally communicated in the first sixty seconds is surface knowledge and insight. Often times a person will dig deeper into the source of frustration or the true cause. If your next question is about the surface info, you may never lead your coachee to the cause. Therefore, you cannot lead him/her to a true path of effective living or change. It is okay to pause. And in many cases you want to assist your coachee in this valuable insight as well. "Before you answer this, take a moment to think on it..."

Repeat back what you hear. Oftentimes the coachee has the answer inside himself. As a coach it is our responsibility to unearth that answer. One of the better tools you can use is to repeat back - in short version – what you hear the coachee saying. Summerize his three minutes into three or four sentences. Repeating what you hear allows the coachee to hear from a different perspective. There will be times when the coachee will back up and retract. "No, not really. That's not what I meant to say." Or I've had coachees say, "Is that what I sound like. I surely didn't mean to..."

On other ocassions hearing you repeat back what the coachee said will allow him to dig deeper in his own thoughts. (Good time for a statement question) As people dig deeper you can guide them to a right conclusion setting the path to greater effectiveness and life change.

Understanding full body communication assists the worthy coach in formulating the right questions to keep the coachee on path. When you see or sense something out of sync, find a way to dig deeper into the conversation at hand. When a person's voice pattern speeds up and signs of excitement appear in the face and hands, take note. Your coachee is likely speaking of something which elevates his passion. Likewise, if her face begins to turn red and you see the palms close, your coachee is heading toward anger. You might need to change gears and ask, "I noticed some flushness in your face and tenseness in your body. What, in your opinion, causes you stress when talking about this subject?" It is okay to shift gears in a coaching conversation.

I had been working as a coach with Pastor John for some time. John is a very good young man with a great heart for God. Our main focus was helping John, "give the ministry away." John had a habit of doing everything himself. And as with anyone trying to do this, some things get dropped, you are spread thin, and burnout can take a toll on your life and ministry. Not to mention you are robbing someone of using their gifts and skills.

Over the months, John had been making good strides of giving the ministry away, delegating to others and allowing other members of his congregation to lead in those areas delegated. On one particular afternoon as we were sitting in his office the discussion was about a newly revised Welcome and Greeting ministry. John had put together a good sized team for his church. A training session was held, where he let a couple other people lead in much of the training (good delegation). This larger group had divided into three separate teams and would rotate manning their positions as the welcoming team on Sunday mornings.

I asked, "What is your next step? What do you need to do next to make this a viable, fruit bearing ministry?"

John stated, "I need to find someone who will make the call (or text) each week to everyone serving the upcoming Sunday morning, to remind them."

"Okay, Good," I said. "Where should that person come from?"

"From inside the ministry team," was John's response.

"Good." I exhorted. "Who's doing it now?"

"I am." Came John's reply.

"You know that you do not need to be doing that? You need to give that away, right?" I retorted with rhetorical and statement questions.

After a couple more back and forth questions and answers between us, John stated that a lady named Ann had offered to take on the responsibility. To which I replied, "Great. Why haven't you turned it over to her?"

"Because," he stated, "Ann has offered to do things like this in the past. And she is good at it – for about 2-3 months. Then she just fades away. And I end up with it again."

I had to give him credit. John had realized a glitch in this person's service abilities. Rather than continue pursuing the original quest, I shifted gears, still in coaching mode and asked, "How are you going to use Ann?" Within only four questions (using the funnel approach) from me, John came up with the answer. "I need to use her for short term events. We have a church picnic coming up in two months. I need to put her in charge of it. And then I can use her for the Christmas..."

He found it. John had realized the inefficiency. Then with four questions he had come to realize how to best utilize this person's gifts and skill set. Now we could move back to the original quest, and we did.

This was not getting side-tracked. I refer to it as coaching in the moment. I realized an opportunity to help this pastor with an issue that directly dealt with our objective as coach and coachee, helping him give the ministry away, to delegate. It is something he remembers to this day and uses in filling positions with the right people.

I find myself coaching in the moment in various areas of my life. I am liable to enter the coaching mode anywhere; sitting as a participant in a Bible study group, in casual conversation, around a restaurant table, even at home with my wife. In fact, this happens quite frequently, I suppose. On occasion, I have not realized I was coaching until my wife has said, "There you go again." Or one of my favorites, "I hate it when you do that." That means I automatically went into coaching mode, broaching a topic that she wanted to talk about, and now realizes coaching will help. Although it also means she did not necessarily want to be coached. But it's fun, and we laugh about it. My point is, once you learn and practice coaching in one area of life, it transcends to other areas as well. When it does, you will also be coaching yourself, and enjoying the outcomes.

There is more to coaching than listening and asking good questions, but as you continue to hone your skills in these two areas, you will become more efficient and effective in your coaching skills and you will see productive development in those you coach. As a worthy coach, you can be effective, in business, ministry, at home, on the sports field, every place and venue in your life. Commit to grow in understanding and practice of the characteristic traits discussed in this book and you will be productive, effective, and respected for your ability to lead others. After all, Coaching, it is a Way of Leadership, a Way of Life!

Appendix

Open-ended Questions

Where do you see yourself in three years?

What could you have done differently?

In your opinion, what are the two greatest needs in our community?

In your opinion, how could a church help meet the needs in our community?

"But what about you, who do you say that I am?"

In your opinion, what makes up a good team?

What are three steps you could take to...?

How could you be better resourced?

In what ways could the church (business) better resource your department?

What can you do this week to you encourage your spouse?

What will it take from you to reach this goal you have set?

In what ways will purchasing that car help you?

If you could go back ten years and give yourself one piece of advice, what would it be?

What do you believe is the most important lesson in the Bible?

What is the most important part of our process as a church/business?

What options do you have in saving for your first home purchase?

Turning Closed-ended questions into Open-ended questions

Closed- Do you enjoy Saturdays?
Open- What does Saturday mean to you?

Closed- Are you happy?

*Open-*What makes you smile? (brings happiness)

Closed- Can I help you with that?
Open- How can I help you with that?

Closed- Are you good working with your hands?
Open- Tell me why you enjoy working with your hands.

Closed- Is that the right answer?
Open- What gives you the assurance this is the right answer?

Rhetorical Questions

Isn't the weather nice today?

Aren't you feeling chipper this morning?

You're not looking to be a failure, are you?

Do you want to be successful?

Are you capable of accomplishing more in this next month?

How much longer can this injustice (behavior, activity) continue?

Statement Questions

You said that you went to work on Tuesday, but didn't stay?

It was definitely Tuesday, right?

The color of this book cover is red, isn't it?

You lived in Enon, Ohio, too?

We pay at the end?

You saw a fox in your front yard?

Our ball team won?

You know that you do not need to be doing that, don't you?

All men are created equal?

Jane likes wearing that blue dress, doesn't she?

Additional Coaching Questions

How should leaders and members share in the responsibility of forward process?

What equipping provisions could be implemented for leaders of your organization?

How can you determine whether a decision is a good decision or the best decision?

How does your church (organization) insure that all wheels are turning in the same direction?

What improvements could be made in the decision making process of your organization?

What would be some benefits of including others?

If you could relieve yourself of three duties (obligations) what would those three be?

How would your life benefit by giving those three obligations away to someone else?

If all obstacles and barriers were removed, what is the one thing you would be doing for God?

What role are you willing to undertake to help your company (church) fulfill its goal?

How will fulfilling this desire (dream) help you in being more effective?

What do you see as an advantageous outcome for your family by proceeding with this course?

How will your friends (or society) benefit by you pursuing this ...?

What are the perceived strengths of your church (organization)?

As an individual, what do you consider to be your strong points?

What would next month look like if...?

Who needs to be included in the discussions to move this forward?

Instead of allowing this to "trickle down", how can you advocate this to members at all levels?

What ramifications or implications do you see if a decision is not made to move forward?

How will those ramifications affect the future ministry of the organization?

How could it benefit you personally if you worked with a team on this project?

Based on our discussion today, what three things will you attempt to accomplish before our next meeting?

Three Questions that can be used in any decision making circumstance

1. If we (I) proceed with this decision, what is the absolute best outcome we can expect?

2. If we (I) proceed with his decision, what is the absolute worst outcome that could happen?

3. Are we (Am I) willing to (can we afford to) live with the outcome of number 2?

---

[i] *The Definitive Book of Body Language*, Bantam Books 2004, Allen & Barbara Pease, page 175

[ii] *Understanding Anger Disorders*, Oxford University Press, Raymond DiGiuseppe, Raymond Chip Tafrate, 2006, pp. 133–159.

[iii] Teaching That Bears Fruit, Guardian Books, 2001, 2007, George L. Yates pages, 71-83

[iv] Teaching That Bears Fruit, Guardian Books, 2001, 2007, George L. Yates, pages 33-37 & 50-53

[v] Teaching That Bears Fruit, Guardian Books, 2001, 2007, George L. Yates

[vi] Merriam Webster's Dictionary, Internet version, 2016

[vii] http://www.mediacollege.com/journalism/interviews/open-ended-questions.html

[viii] Teaching That Bears Fruit, Guardian Books, 2001, 2007, George L. Yates, pages 71-83

62641284R00068

Made in the USA
Lexington, KY
14 April 2017